mini
7
EZ PLAY TODAY
FOR ORGANS, PIANOS &
ELECTRONIC KEYBOARDS

Hallelujah
& 40 More Great Songs

ISBN 978-1-4950-7724-1

HAL•LEONARD®

7777 W. Bluemound Rd. P.O. Box 13819 Milwaukee, WI 53213

Visit Hal Leonard Online at
www.halleonard.com

Ain't No Sunshine

Registration 8
Rhythm: 8-Beat or Blues

Words and Music by
Bill Withers

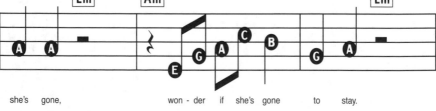

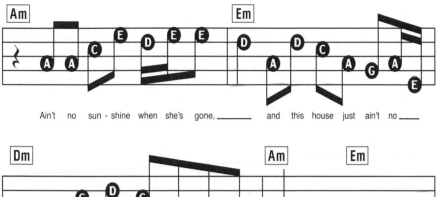

Ain't no sun-shine when she's gone, _____ and this house just ain't no _____

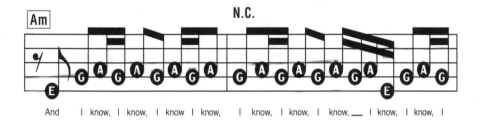

home _____ an - y time she goes a - way.

And I know, I know, I know I know, I know, I know, I know, __ I know, I know, I

know, I know, I know, __ I know, I know, I know, I know I know, I know, I know, I know,

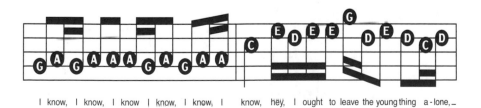

I know, I know, I know I know, I know, I know, hey, I ought to leave the young thing a - lone, __

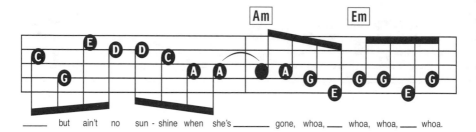

_____ but ain't no sun - shine when she's _____ gone, whoa, _____ whoa, whoa, _____ whoa.

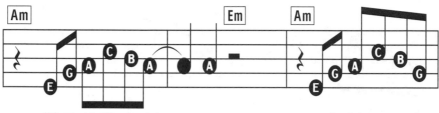

Ain't no sun - shine when she's _____ gone, on - ly dark - ness ev - 'ry

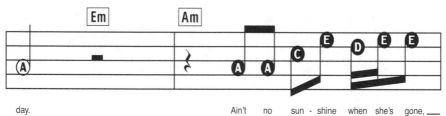

day. Ain't no sun - shine when she's gone, _____

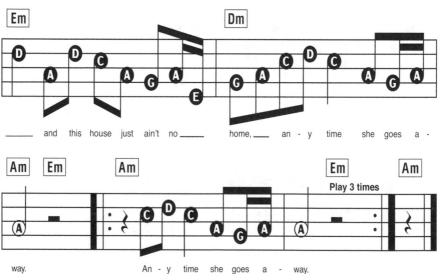

_____ and this house just ain't no _____ home, _____ an - y time she goes a -

way. An - y time she goes a - way.

Cecilia

Registration 9
Rhythm: March or Rock

Words and Music by
Paul Simon

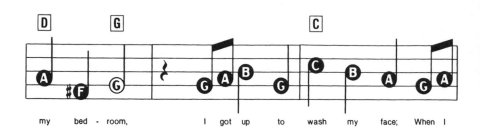

my bed - room, I got up to wash my face; When I

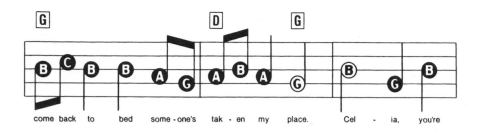

come back to bed some - one's tak - en my place. Cel - ia, you're

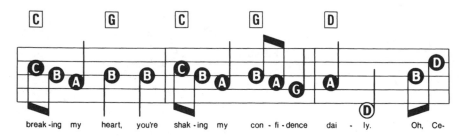

break -ing my heart, you're shak -ing my con - fi -dence dai - ly. Oh, Ce-

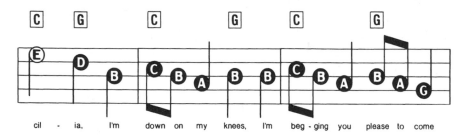

cil - ia, I'm down on my knees, I'm beg -ging you please to come

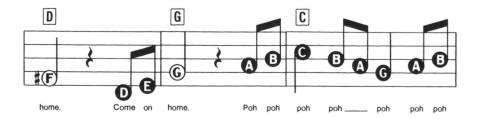

home. Come on home. Poh poh poh poh _____ poh poh poh

9

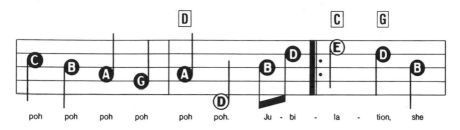

poh poh poh poh poh poh. Ju - bi - la - tion, she

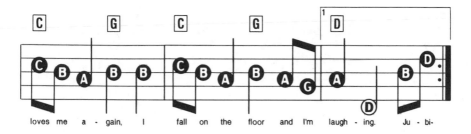

loves me a - gain, I fall on the floor and I'm laugh - ing. Ju - bi-

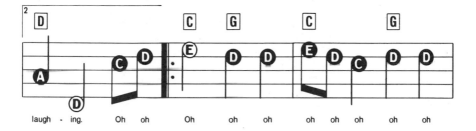

laugh - ing. Oh oh Oh oh oh oh oh oh oh oh

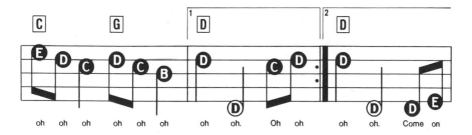

oh oh oh oh oh oh oh oh. Oh oh oh oh. Come on

home.

Alone Together

Registration 2
Rhythm: Ballad

Lyrics by Howard Dietz
Music by Arthur Schwartz

11

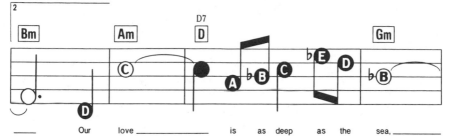

Our love _____ is as deep as the sea, _____

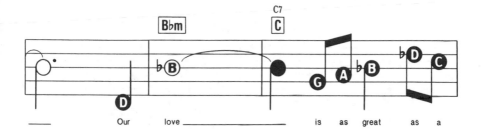

Our love _____ is as great as a

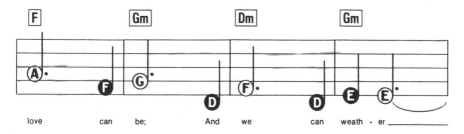

love can be; And we can weath-er _____

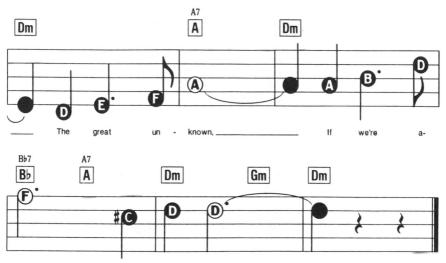

_____ The great un - known, _____ If we're a-

lone to - geth - er. _____

Blue Moon

Registration 8
Rhythm: Swing

Music by Richard Rodgers
Lyrics by Lorenz Hart

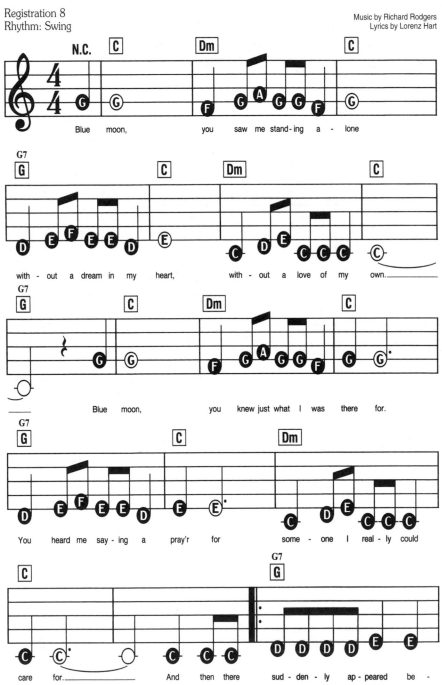

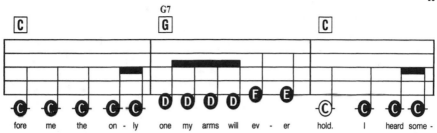

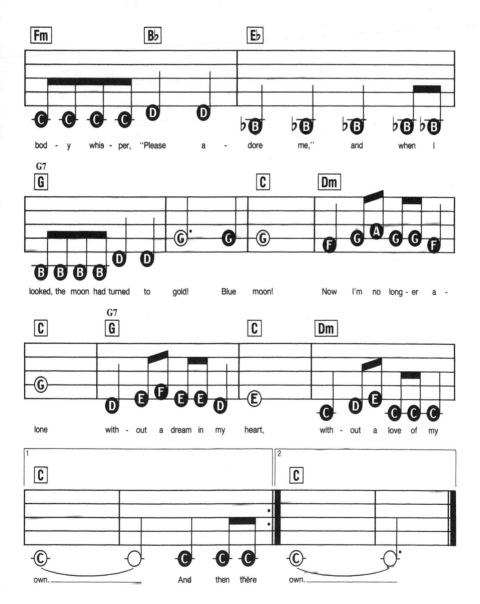

Chattanooga Choo Choo

Registration 9
Rhythm: Swing

Words by Mack Gordon
Music by Harry Warren

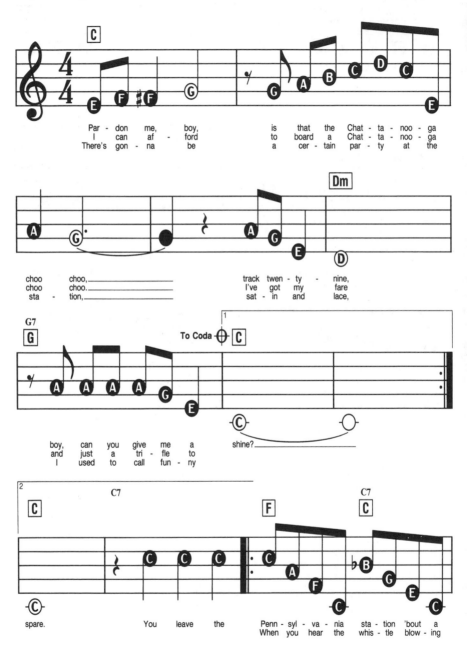

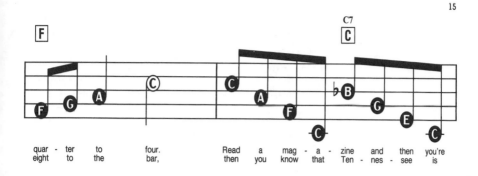

quar - ter to four. Read a mag - a - zine and then you're
eight to the bar, then you know that Ten - nes - see is

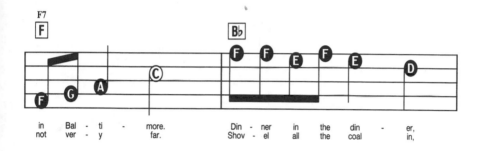

in Bal - ti - more. Din - ner in the din - er,
not ver - y far. Shov - el all the coal in,

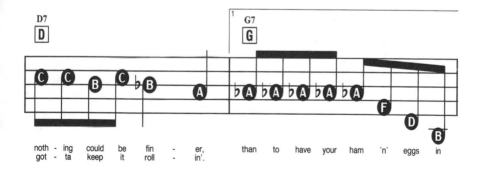

noth - ing could be fin - er, than to have your ham 'n' eggs in
got - ta keep it roll - in'.

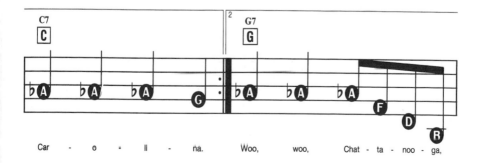

Car - o - li - na. Woo, woo, Chat - ta - noo - ga,

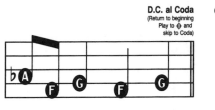

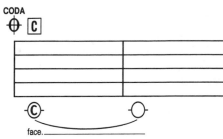

there___ you are.___ face.___

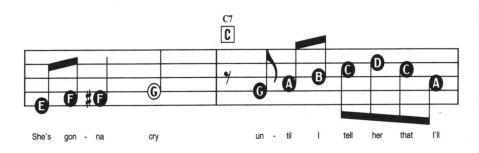

She's gon - na cry un - til I tell her that I'll

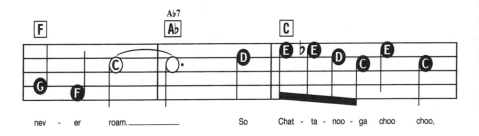

nev - er roam.___ So Chat - ta - noo - ga choo choo,

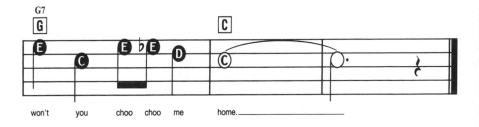

won't you choo choo me home.___

Do You Believe in Magic

Registration 4
Rhythm: Country

Words and Music by
John Sebastian

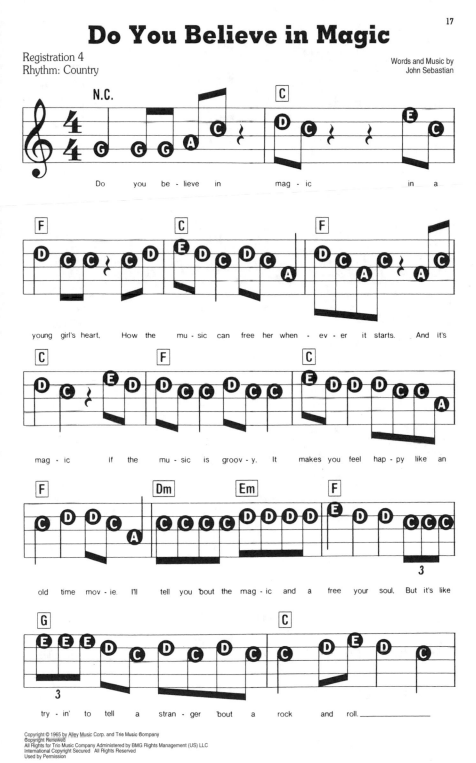

18

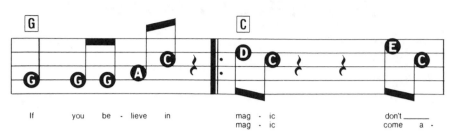

If you be - lieve in mag - ic don't _____
mag - ic come a -

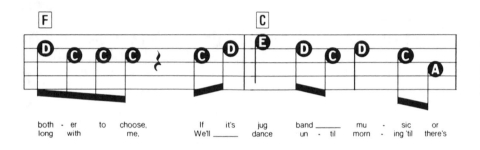

both - er to choose, If it's jug band _____ mu - sic or
long with me. We'll _____ dance un - til morn - ing 'til there's

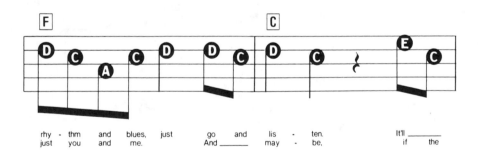

rhy - thm and blues, just go and lis - ten. It'll _____
just you and me. And _____ may - be, if the

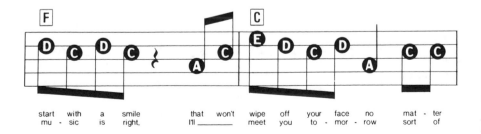

start with a smile that won't wipe off your face no mat - ter
mu - sic is right, I'll _____ meet you to - mor - row sort of

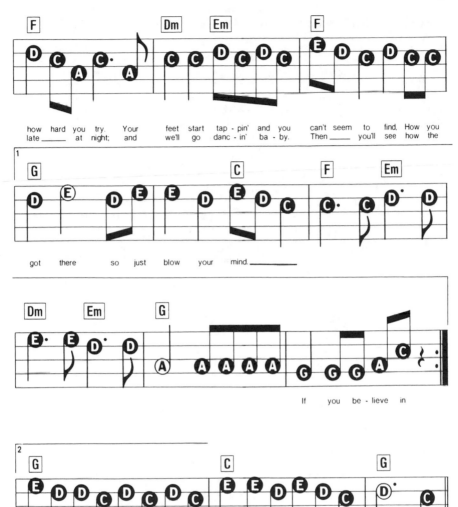

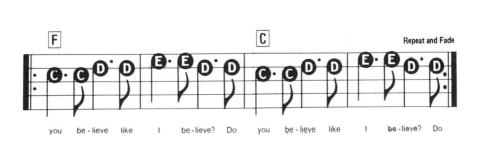

Emily
from the MGM Motion Picture THE AMERICANIZATION OF EMILY

Registration 3
Rhythm: Waltz

Music by Johnny Mandel
Words by Johnny Mercer

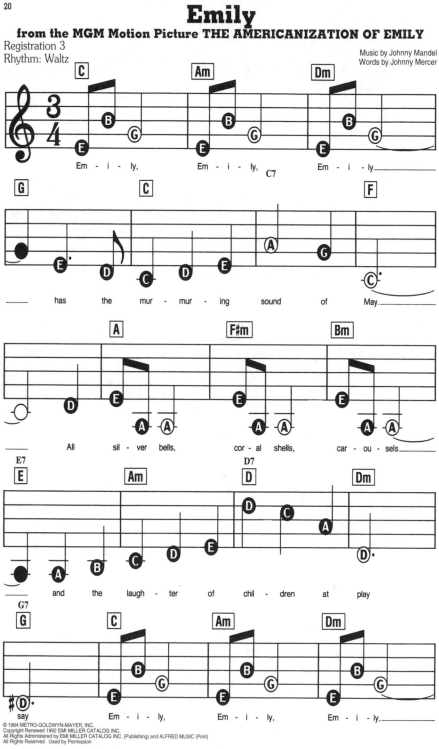

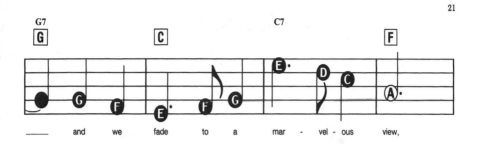

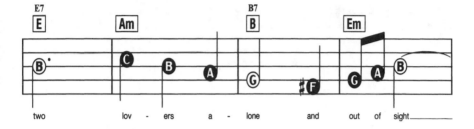

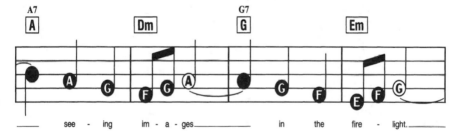

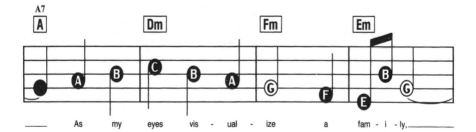

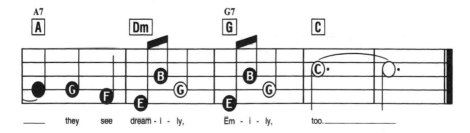

Hallelujah

Registration 4
Rhythm: 6/8 March

Words and Music by
Leonard Cohen

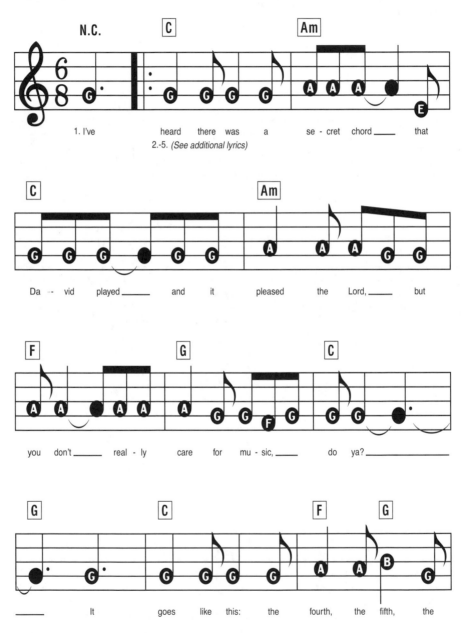

1. I've heard there was a se - cret chord ___ that

2.-5. *(See additional lyrics)*

Da - vid played ___ and it pleased the Lord, ___ but

you don't ___ real - ly care for mu - sic, ___ do ya? ___

___ It goes like this: the fourth, the fifth, the

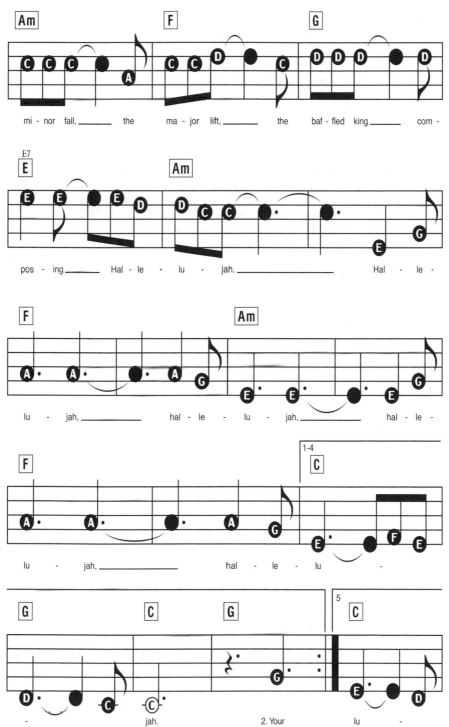

mi - nor fall, _____ the ma - jor lift, _____ the baf - fled king _____ com -

pos - ing _____ Hal - le - lu - jah. _____ Hal - le -

lu - jah, _____ hal - le - lu - jah, _____ hal - le -

lu - jah, _____ hal - le - lu -

- jah. 2. Your lu -

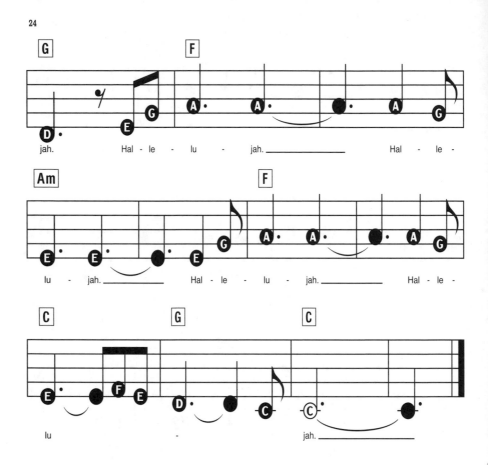

jah.   Hal - le - lu - jah. _____ Hal - le -

lu - jah. _____ Hal - le - lu - jah. _____ Hal - le -

lu - jah. _____

Additional Lyrics

2. Your faith was strong but you needed proof.
   You saw her bathing on the roof.
   Her beauty and the moonlight overthrew ya.
   She tied you to a kitchen chair.
   She broke your throne, she cut your hair.
   And from your lips she drew the Hallelujah.

3. Maybe I have been here before.
   I know this room, I've walked this floor.
   I used to live alone before I knew ya.
   I've seen your flag on the marble arch.
   Love is not a vict'ry march.
   It's a cold and it's a broken Hallelujah.

4. There was a time you let me know
   What's real and going on below.
   But now you never show it to me, do ya?
   And remember when I moved in you.
   The holy dark was movin', too,
   And every breath we drew was Hallelujah.

5. Maybe there's a God above,
   And all I ever learned from love
   Was how to shoot at someone who outdrew ya.
   And it's not a cry you can hear at night.
   It's not somebody who's seen the light.
   It's a cold and it's a broken Hallelujah.

Happy Days Are Here Again

Registration 2
Rhythm: Fox Trot or Swing

Words and Music by Jack Yellen
and Milton Ager

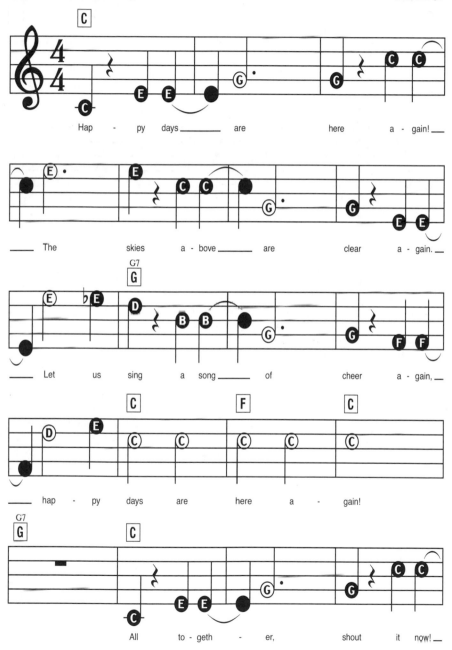

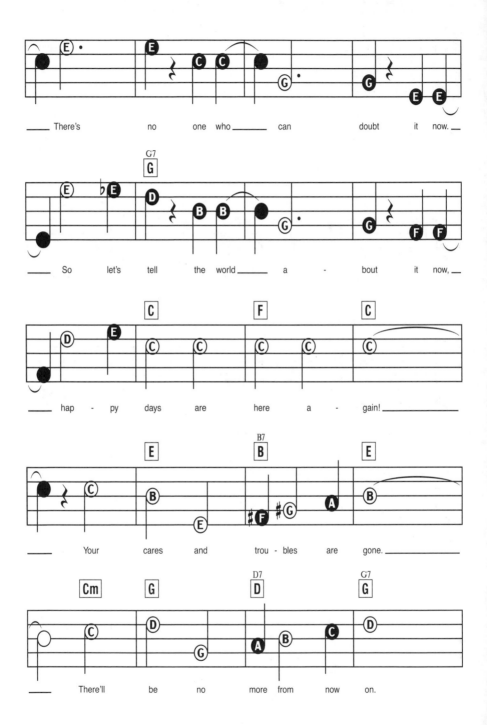

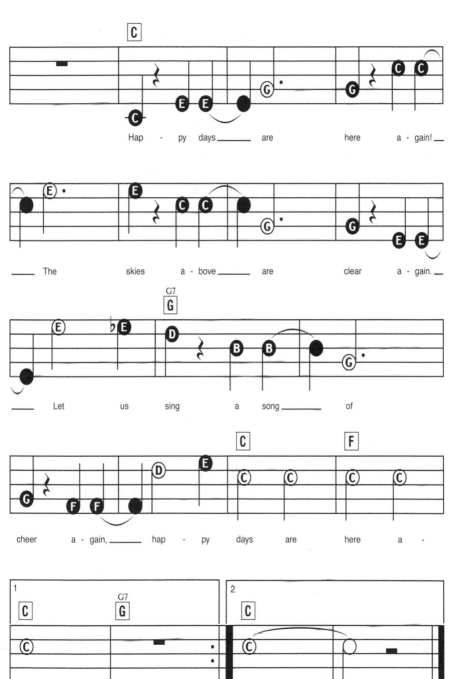

Hey There
from THE PAJAMA GAME

Registration 2
Rhythm: Fox Trot

Words and Music by Richard Adler
and Jerry Ross

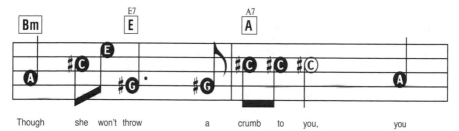

Though she won't throw a crumb to you, you

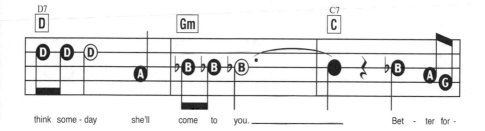

think some - day she'll come to you. _____ Bet - ter for -

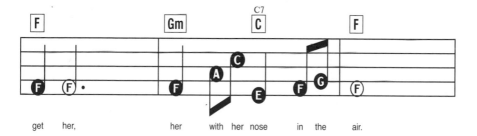

get her, her with her nose in the air.

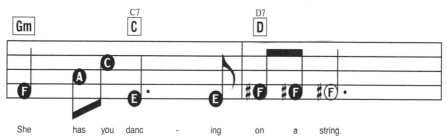

She has you danc - ing on a string.

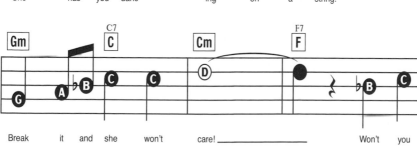

Break it and she won't care! _____ Won't you

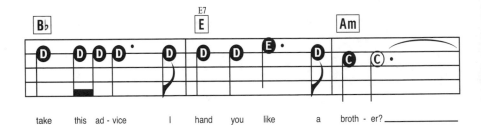

take this ad - vice I hand you like a broth - er? _____

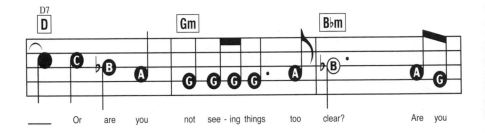

_____ Or are you not see - ing things too clear? Are you

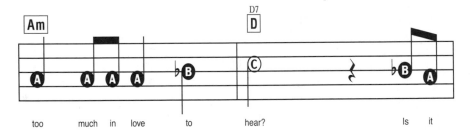

too much in love to hear? Is it

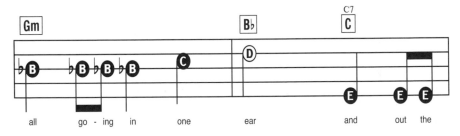

all go - ing in one ear and out the

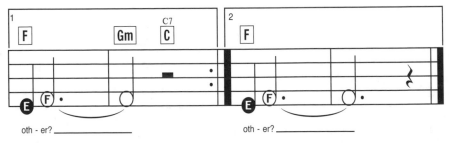

oth - er? _____   oth - er? _____

I Got You Babe

Registration 5
Rhythm: Slow Rock or 12-Beat

Words and Music by
Sonny Bono

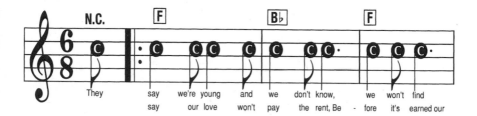

They
say   we're young   and   we   don't know,   we   won't find

say   our love   won't   pay   the rent, Be - fore   it's   earned our

out _____ till   we   grow,   Well   I   don't know   if

mon - ey's   all   been   spent.   I   guess   that's so,   we

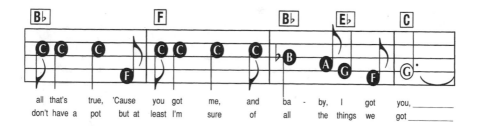

all   that's   true,   'Cause   you got   me,   and   ba - by,   I   got   you, _____

don't have a   pot   but at   least I'm   sure   of   all   the things   we   got _____

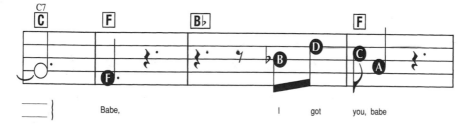

_____ }   Babe,   I   got   you, babe

32

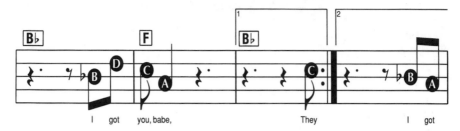

I got   you, babe,   They   I   got

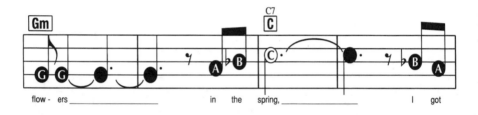

flow - ers _____   in   the   spring, _____   I   got

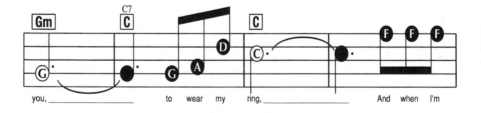

you, _____   to   wear   my   ring, _____   And when I'm

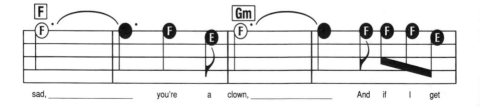

sad, _____   you're   a   clown, _____   And if   I   get

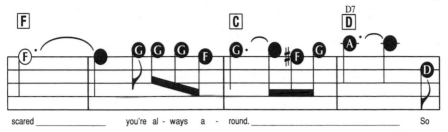

scared _____ you're al - ways a - round. _____ So

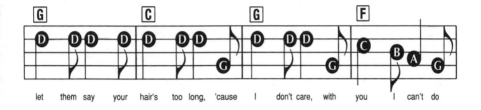

let them say your hair's too long, 'cause I don't care, with you I can't do

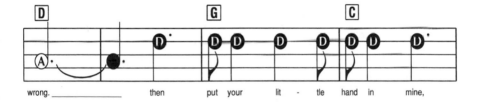

wrong. _____ then put your lit - tle hand in mine,

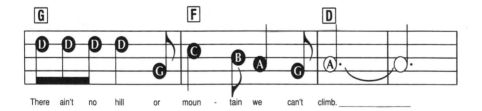

There ain't no hill or moun - tain we can't climb. _____

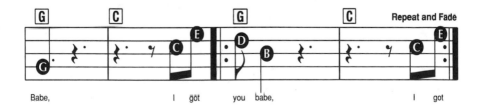

Babe, I got you babe, I got

The House of the Rising Sun

Registration 4
Rhythm: Waltz

Words and Music by
Alan Price

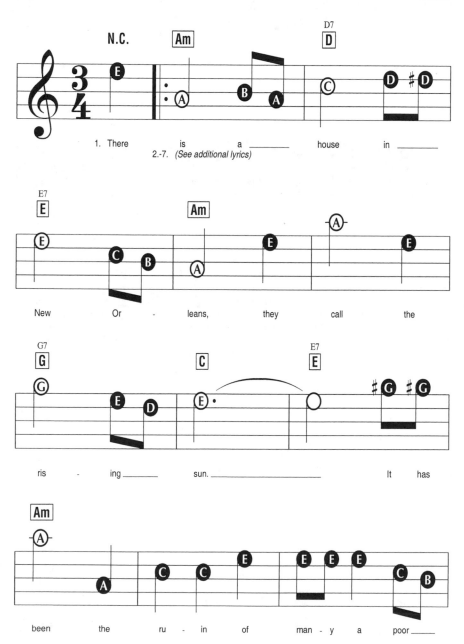

1. There   is   a _____ house   in _____
2.-7. *(See additional lyrics)*

New   Or - leans,   they   call   the

ris - ing _____ sun. _____ It   has

been   the   ru - in   of   man - y   a   poor _____

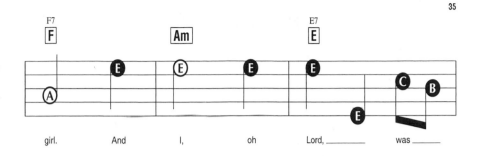

girl.　　　And　　　I,　　　oh　　　Lord,＿＿＿＿　was＿＿＿＿

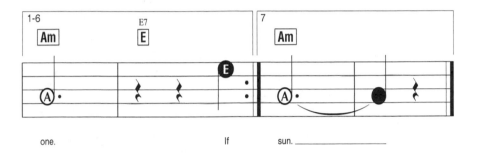

one.　　　　　　　　　If　　　sun.＿＿＿＿＿＿＿

Additional Lyrics

2. If I had listened to what mama said,
I'd 'a' been at home today.
Being so young and foolish, poor girl,
Let a gambler lead me astray.

3. My mother, she's a tailor,
She sells those new blue jeans.
My sweetheart, he's a drunkard, Lord,
Drinks down in New Orleans.

4. The only thing a drunkard needs
Is a suitcase and a trunk.
The only time he's satisfied
Is when he's on a drunk.

5. Go tell my baby, sister,
Never do like I have done.
To shun that house in New Orleans,
They call the Rising Sun.

6. One foot is on the platform,
And the other one on the train.
I'm going back to New Orleans
To wear that ball and chain.

7. I'm going back to New Orleans,
My race is almost run.
Going back to end my life
Beneath the rising sun.

How About You?

Registration 9
Rhythm: Swing

Words by Ralph Freed
Music by Burton Lane

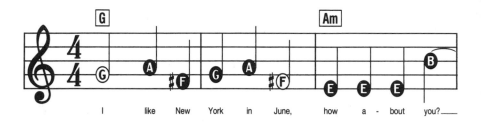

I like New York in June, how a - bout you?

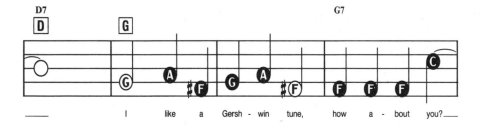

_____ I like a Gersh - win tune, how a - bout you? _____

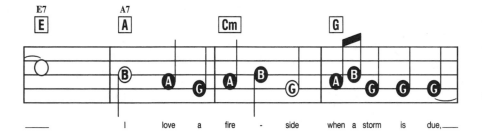

_____ I love a fire - side when a storm is due, _____

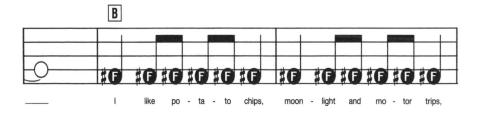

_____ I like po - ta - to chips, moon - light and mo - tor trips,

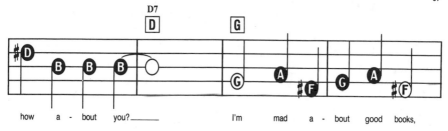

how a - bout you?_____ I'm mad a - bout good books,

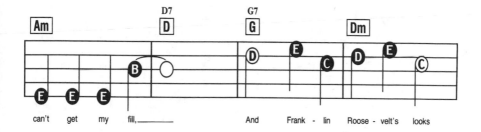

can't get my fill,_____ And Frank - lin Roose - velt's looks

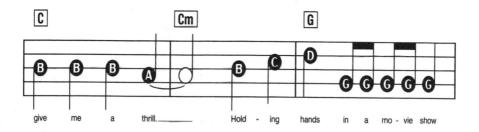

give me a thrill._____ Hold - ing hands in a mo - vie show

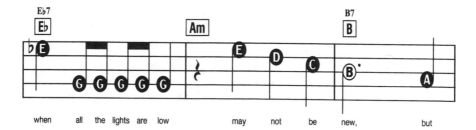

when all the lights are low may not be new, but

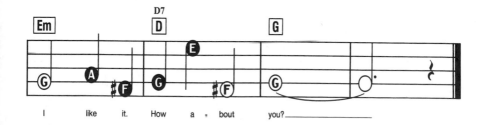

I like it. How a - bout you?_____

I Only Have Eyes for You

Registration 3
Rhythm: Fox Trot or Swing

Words by Al Dubin
Music by Harry Warren

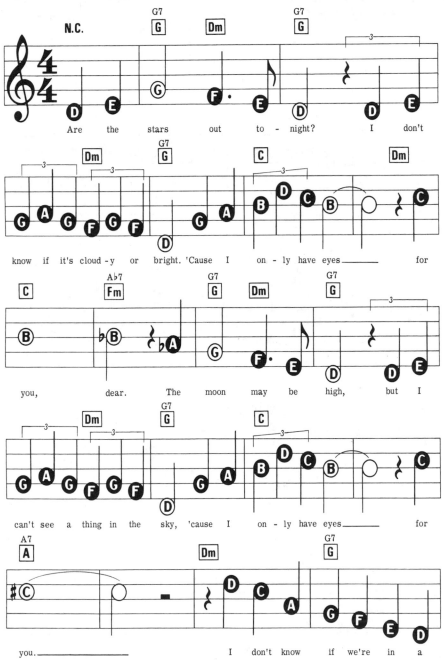

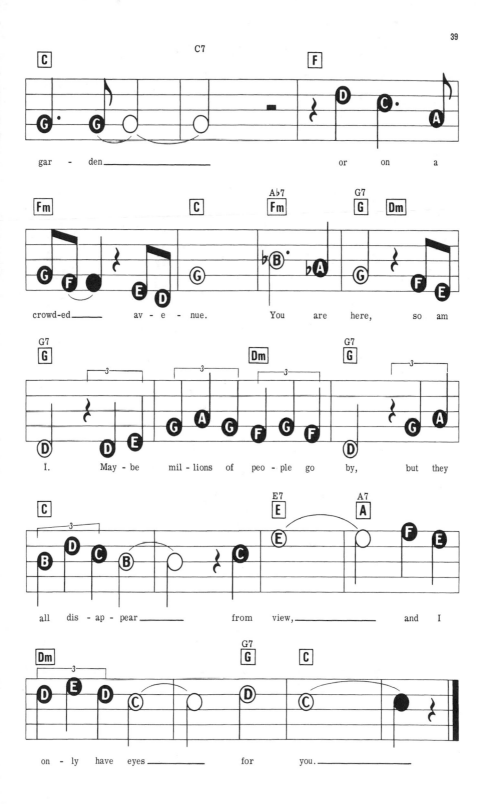

I'm in the Mood for Love

Registration 9
Rhythm: Fox Trot or Pops

Words and Music by Jimmy McHugh
and Dorothy Fields

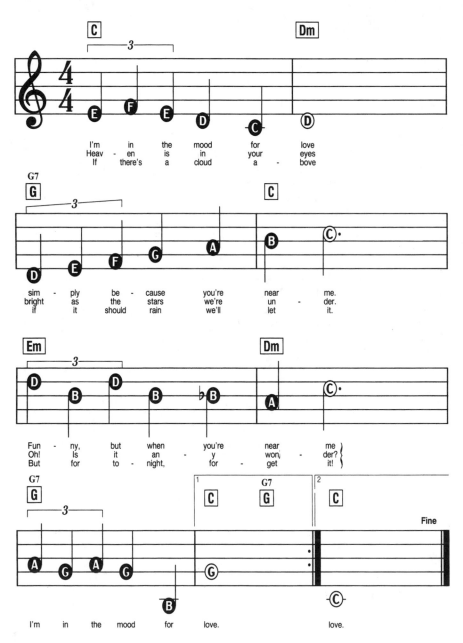

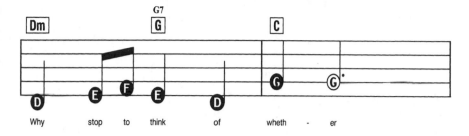

Why   stop   to   think   of   wheth - er

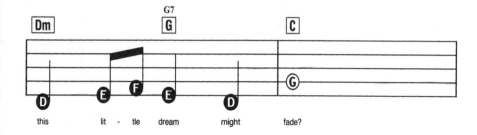

this   lit - tle   dream   might   fade?

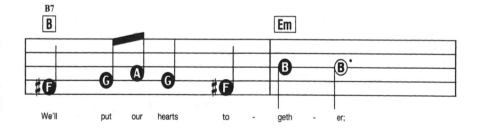

We'll   put   our   hearts   to - geth - er;

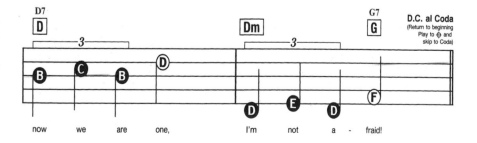

now   we   are   one,   I'm   not   a - fraid!

D.C. al Coda
(Return to beginning
Play to ⊕ and
skip to Coda)

Isn't She Lovely

Registration 8
Rhythm: Swing or Shuffle

Words and Music by
Stevie Wonder

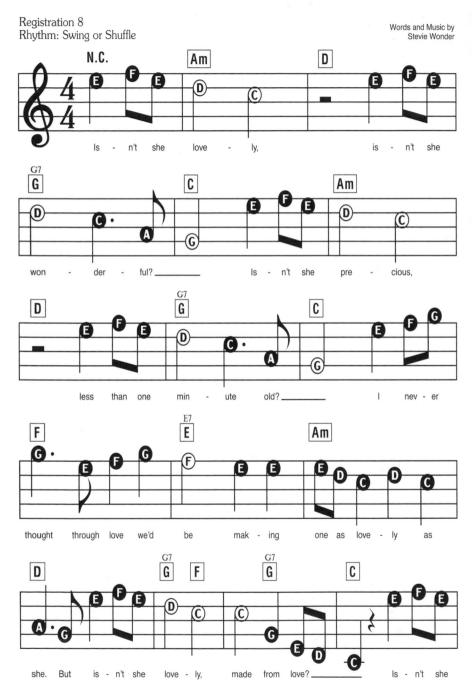

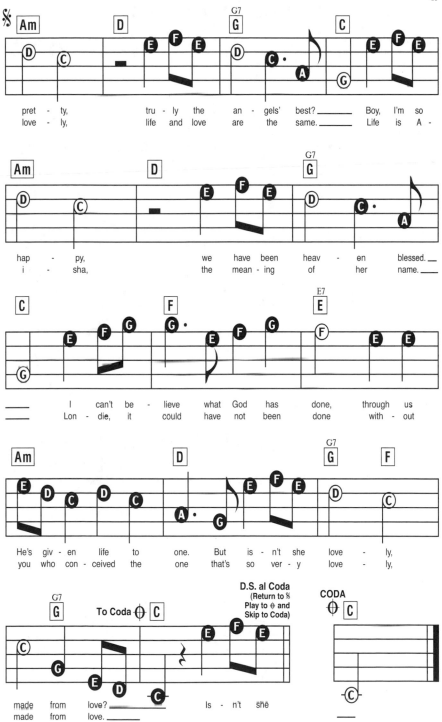

It Had to Be You

Registration 9
Rhythm: Swing

Words by Gus Kahn
Music by Isham Jones

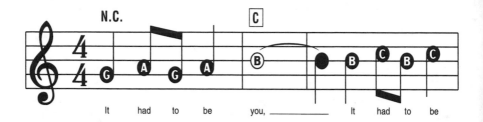

It had to be you, _____ It had to be

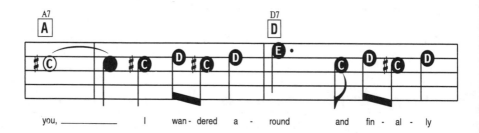

you, _____ I wan - dered a - round and fin - al - ly

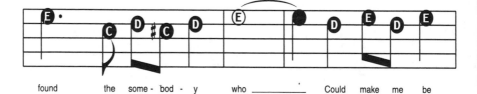

found the some - bod - y who _____ Could make me be

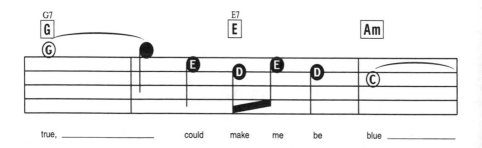

true, _____ could make me be blue _____

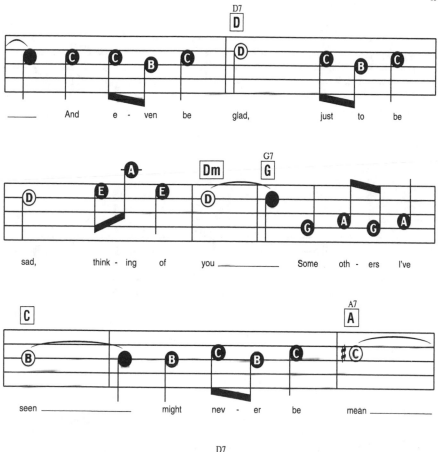

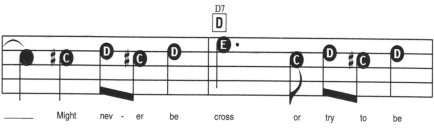

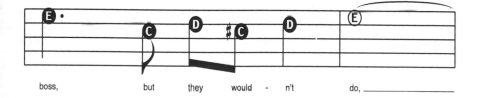

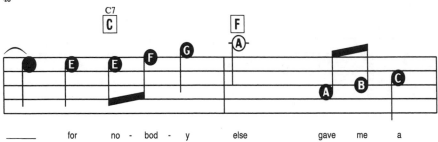

_____ for no - bod - y else gave me a

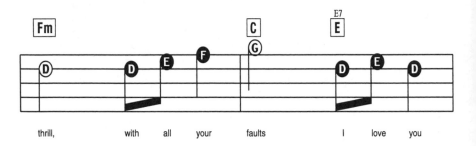

thrill, with all your faults I love you

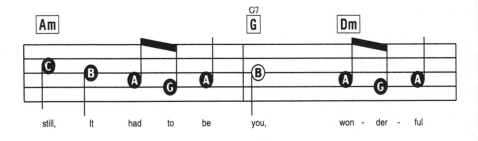

still, It had to be you, won - der - ful

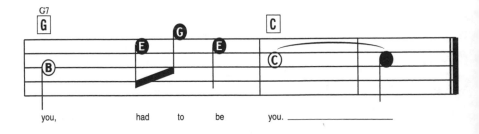

you, had to be you. _____

Man in the Mirror

Registration 5
Rhythm: Rock

Words and Music by Glen Ballard
and Siedah Garrett

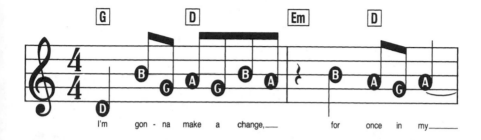

I'm gon-na make a change,___ for once in my___

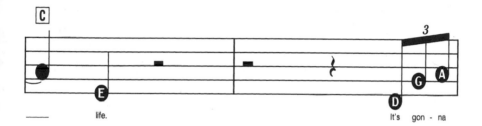

___ life. It's gon-na

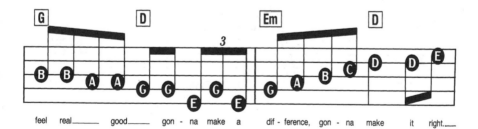

feel real___ good___ gon-na make a dif-ference, gon-na make it right.___

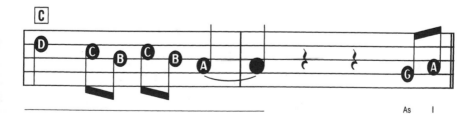

As I

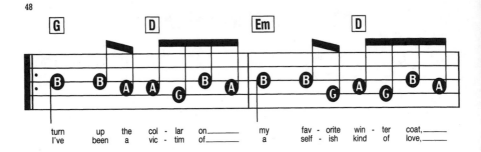

turn up the col - lar on_____ my fav - orite win - ter coat,_____
I've been a vic - tim of_____ a self - ish kind of love,_____

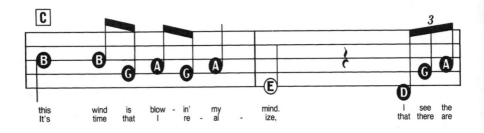

this wind is blow - in' my mind. I see the
It's time that I re - al - ize, that there are

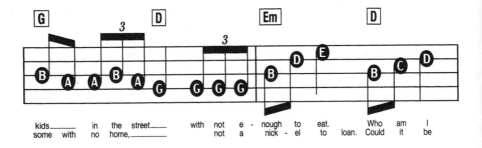

kids_____ in the street_____ with not e - nough to eat. Who am I
some with no home,_____ not a nick - el to loan. Could it be

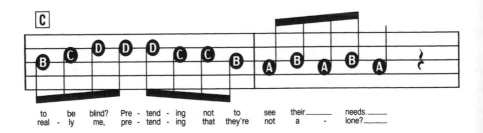

to be blind? Pre - tend - ing not to see their_____ needs._____
real - ly me, pre - tend - ing that they're not a - lone?_____

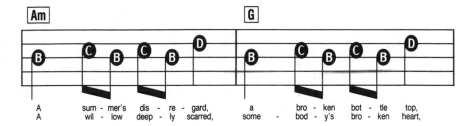

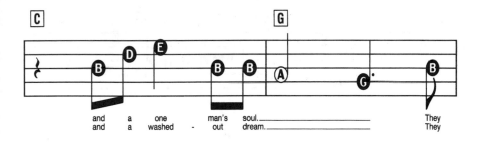

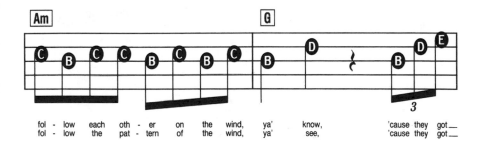

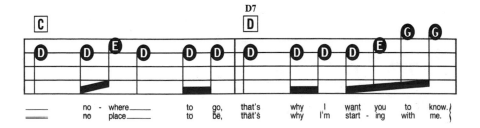

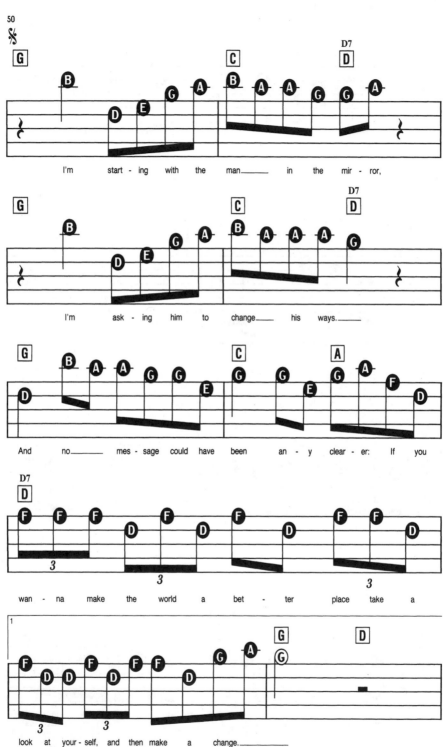

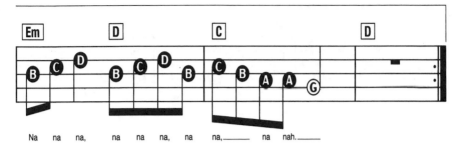

Na na na, na na na, na na,_____ na nah._____

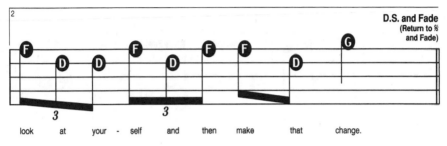

D.S. and Fade
(Return to 𝄋
and Fade)

look at your-self and then make that change.

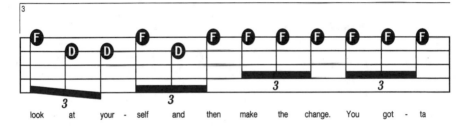

look at your-self and then make the change. You got - ta

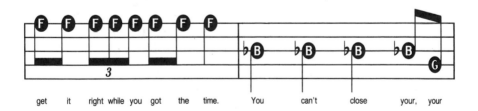

get it right while you got the time. You can't close your, your

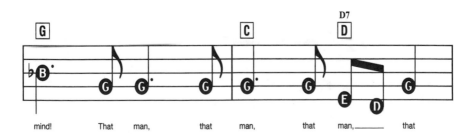

mind! That man, that man, that man,_____ that

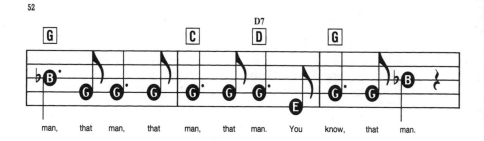

man, that man, that man, that man. You know, that man.

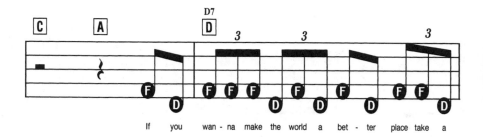

If you wan - na make the world a bet - ter place take a

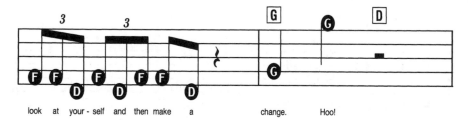

look at your - self and then make a change. Hoo!

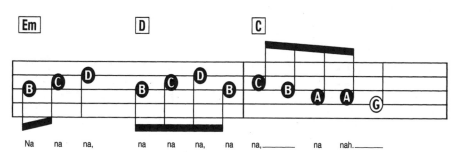

Na na na, na na na, na na, na nah.

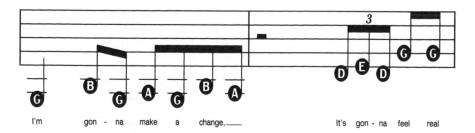

I'm gon - na make a change, It's gon - na feel real

good! Come on! Just lift your -

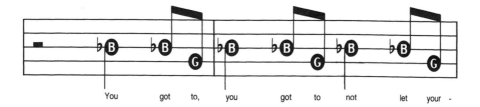

self, you know. You've got to stop it. Your -

self! I've got to make that change, to - day! Hoo!

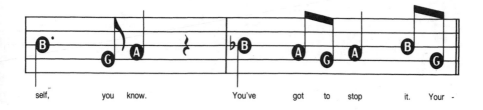

You got to, you got to not let your -

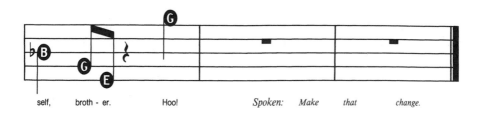

self, broth - er. Hoo! *Spoken: Make that change.*

Jeepers Creepers

Registration 1
Rhythm: Fox Trot or Swing

Words by Johnny Mercer
Music by Harry Warren

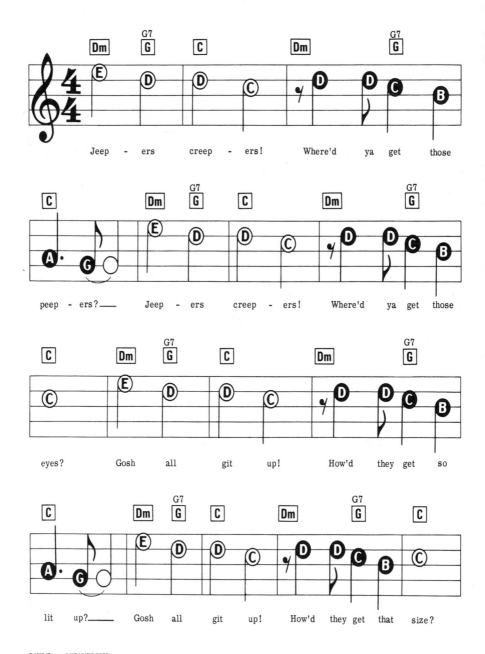

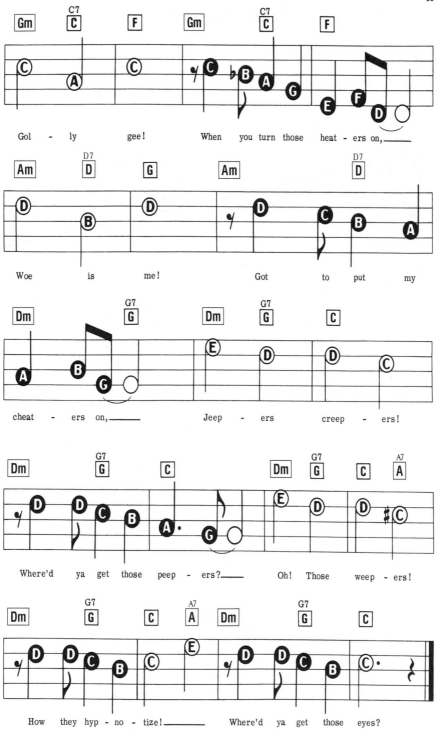

56

Just Friends

Registration 1
Rhythm: Swing or Fox Trot

Lyrics by Sam M. Lewis
Music by John Klenner

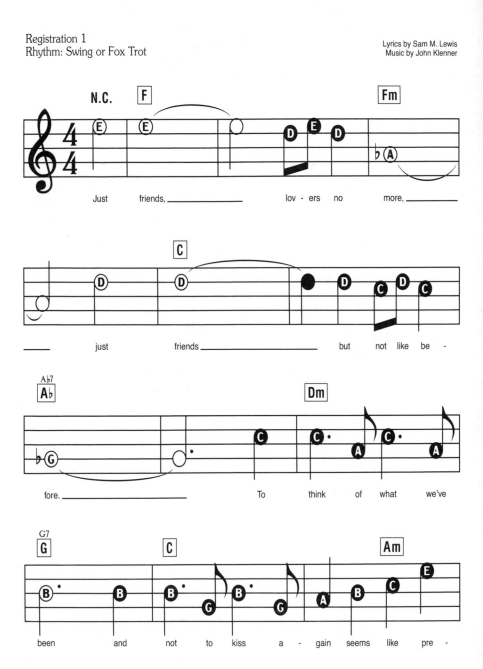

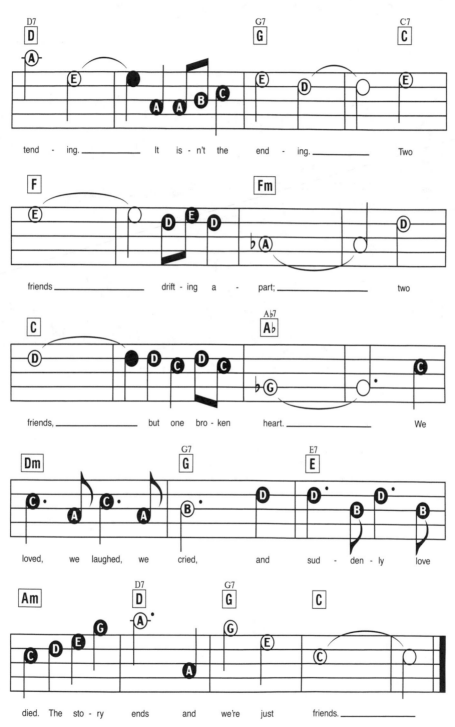

A Kiss to Build a Dream On

Registration 8
Rhythm: Swing or Fox Trot

Words and Music by Bert Kalmar,
Harry Ruby and Oscar Hammerstein II

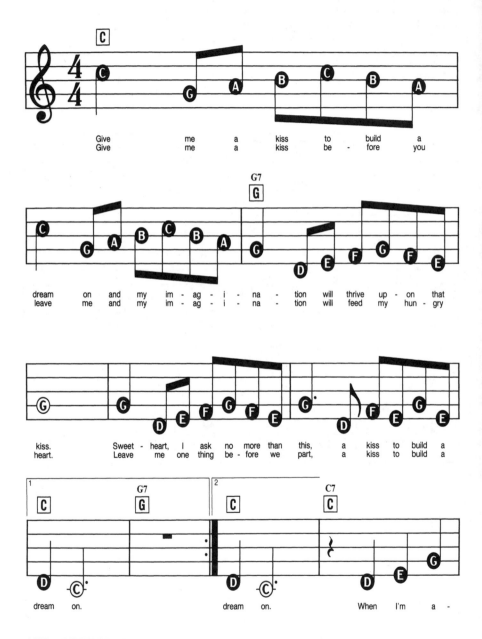

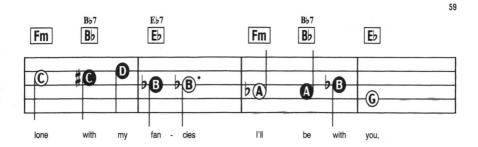

lone with my fan - cies I'll be with you,

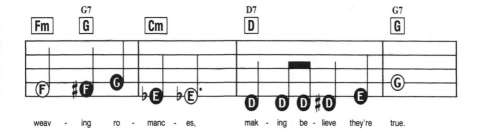

weav - ing ro - manc - es, mak - ing be - lieve they're true.

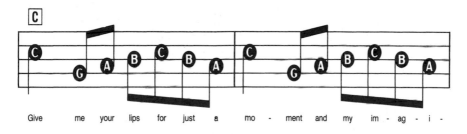

Give me your lips for just a mo - ment and my im - ag - i -

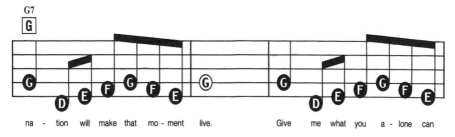

na - tion will make that mo - ment live. Give me what you a - lone can

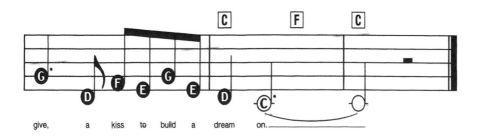

give, a kiss to build a dream on. _____

Knockin' on Heaven's Door

Registration 4
Rhythm: 8-Beat or Rock

Words and Music by
Bob Dylan

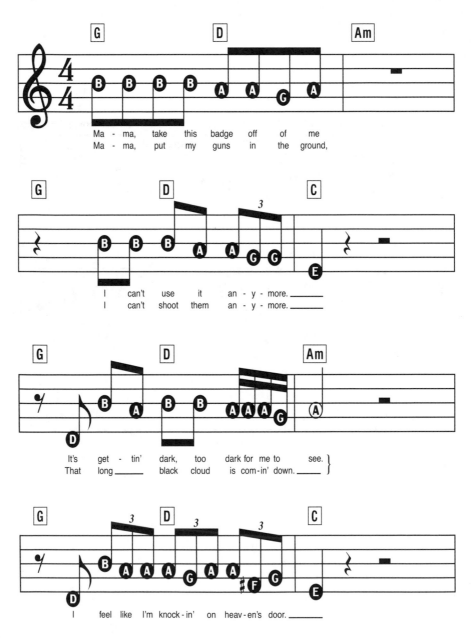

Ma - ma, take this badge off of me
Ma - ma, put my guns in the ground,

I can't use it an - y - more.
I can't shoot them an - y - more.

It's get - tin' dark, too dark for me to see.
That long____ black cloud is com - in' down.____

I feel like I'm knock - in' on heav - en's door.____

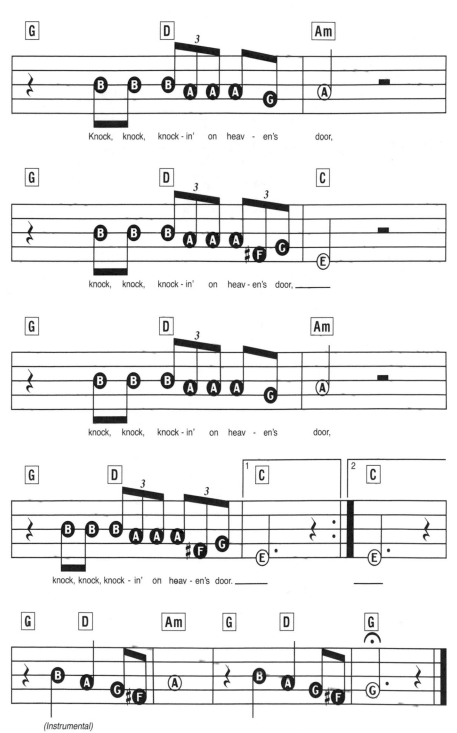

Knock, knock, knock - in' on heav - en's door,

knock, knock, knock - in' on heav - en's door, _____

knock, knock, knock - in' on heav - en's door,

knock, knock, knock - in' on heav - en's door. _____   _____

(Instrumental)

Moondance

Registration 2
Rhythm: Shuffle

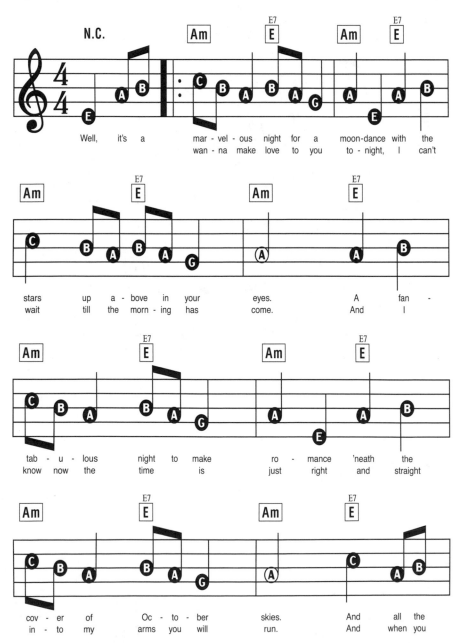

Well, it's a mar - vel - ous night for a moon-dance with the
wan - na make love to you to - night, I can't

stars up a - bove in your eyes. A fan -
wait till the morn - ing has come. And I

tab - u - lous night to make ro - mance 'neath the
know now the time is just right and straight

cov - er of Oc - to - ber skies. And all the
in - to my arms you will run. And when you

64

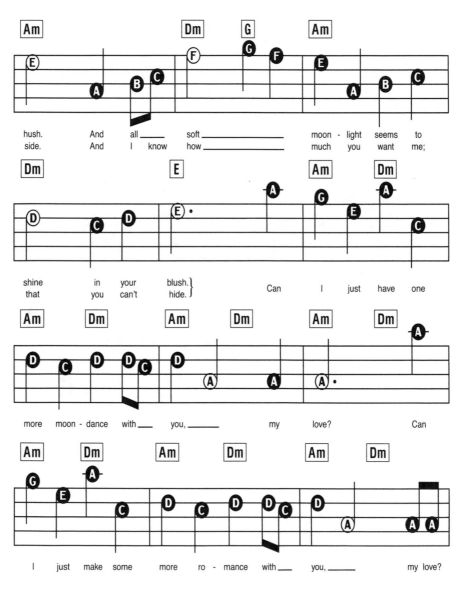

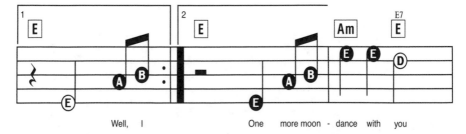

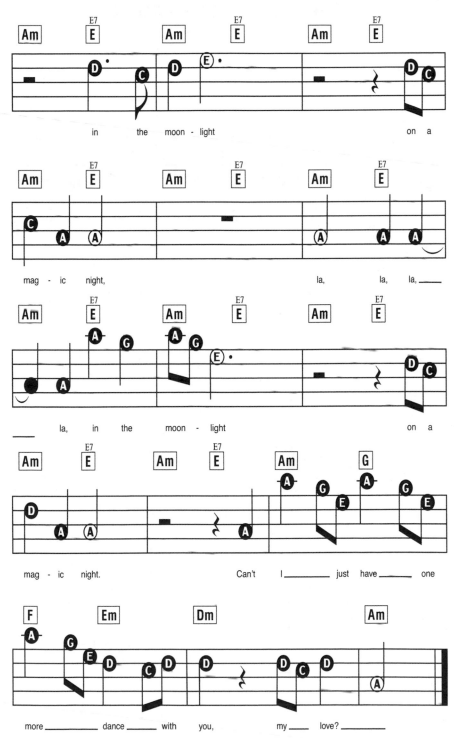

Moonlight Serenade

Registration 9
Rhythm: Swing or Big Band

Words by Mitchell Parish
Music by Glen Miller

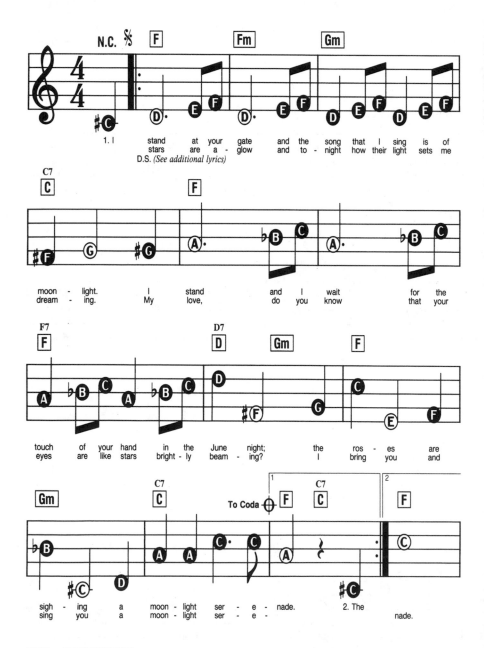

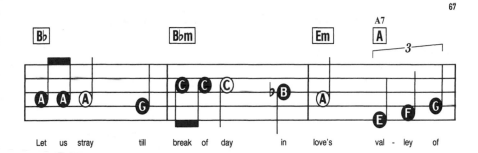

Let us stray till break of day in love's val - ley of

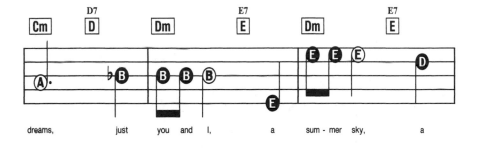

dreams, just you and I, a sum - mer sky, a

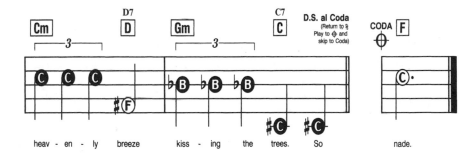

heav - en - ly breeze kiss - ing the trees. So nade.

Additional Lyrics

D.S.   So don't let me wait,
come to me tenderly in the June night.
I stand at your gate
and I sing you a song in the moonlight;
a love song, my darling,
a moonlight serenade.

Pennies from Heaven

Registration 2
Rhythm: Fox Trot or Swing

Words by John Burke
Music by Arthur Johnston

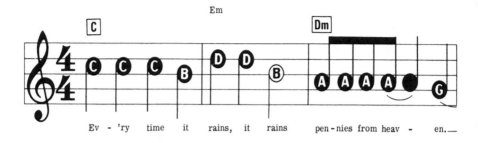

Ev - 'ry time it rains, it rains pen - nies from heav - en.

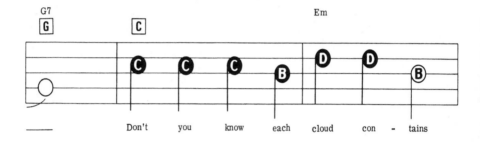

_____ Don't you know each cloud con - tains

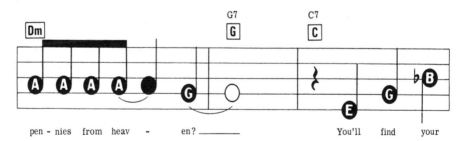

pen - nies from heav - en? _____ You'll find your

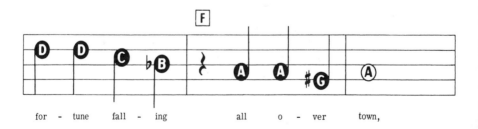

for - tune fall - ing all o - ver town,

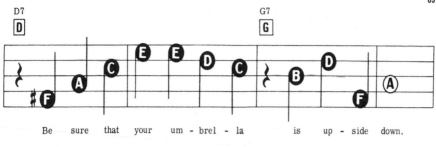

Be sure that your um - brel - la is up - side down.

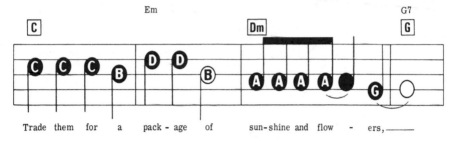

Trade them for a pack - age of sun-shine and flow - ers,_____

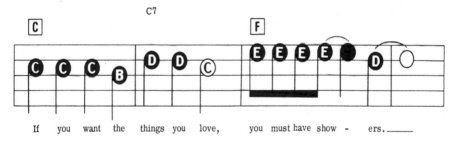

If you want the things you love, you must have show - ers._____

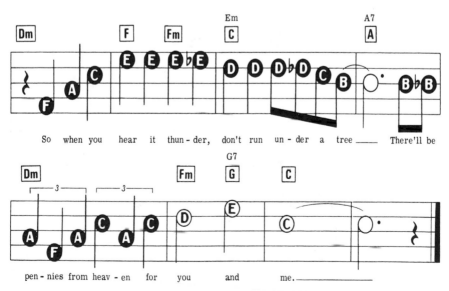

So when you hear it thun - der, don't run un - der a tree ____ There'll be

pen - nies from heav - en for you and me._____

People Get Ready

Registration 1
Rhythm: 4/4 Ballad or 8-Beat

Words and Music by
Curtis Mayfield

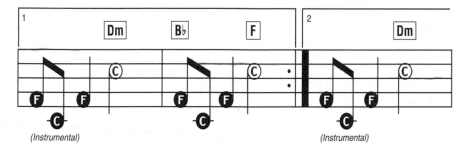

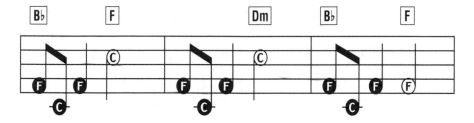

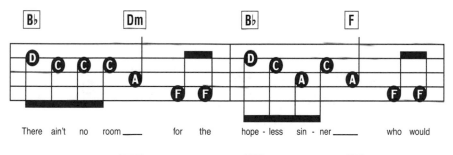

There ain't no room ___ for the hope-less sin-ner ___ who would

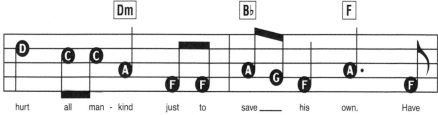

hurt all man-kind just to save ___ his own, Have

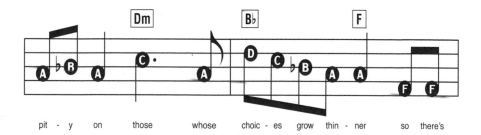

pit - y on those whose choic-es grow thin-ner so there's

72

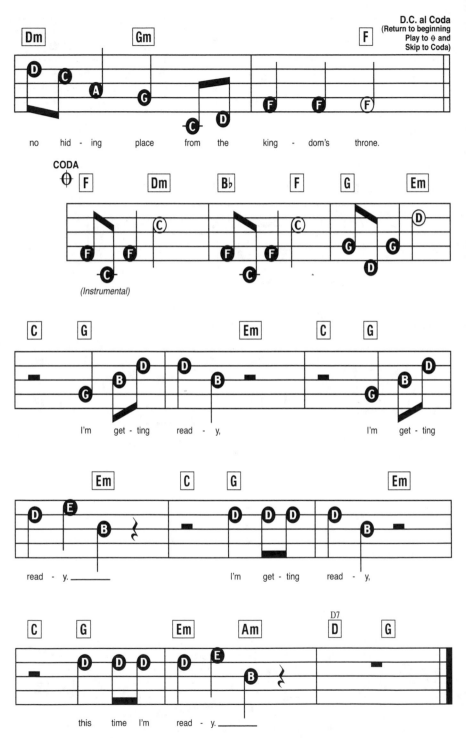

That's All

Registration 10
Rhythm: Ballad

Words and Music by Bob Haymes
and Alan E. Brandt

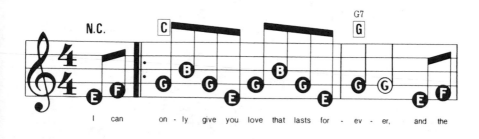

I can on-ly give you love that lasts for-ev-er, and the

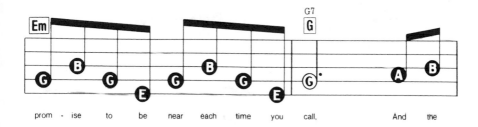

prom-ise to be near each time you call, And the

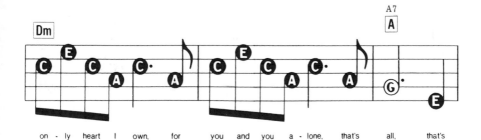

on-ly heart I own, for you and you a-lone, that's all, that's

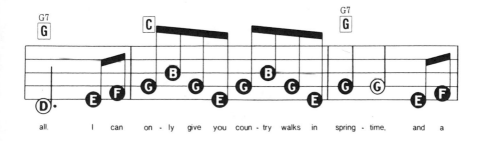

all. I can on-ly give you coun-try walks in spring-time, and a

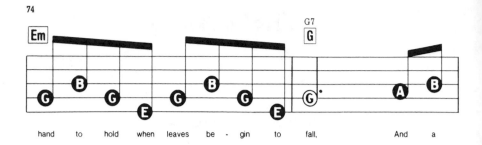

hand   to   hold   when   leaves   be - gin   to   fall,   And   a

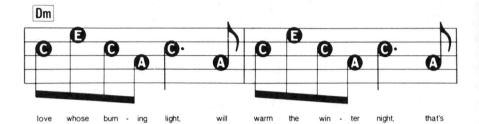

love   whose   burn - ing   light,   will   warm   the   win - ter   night,   that's

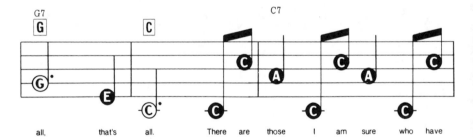

all,   that's   all.   There   are   those   I   am   sure   who   have

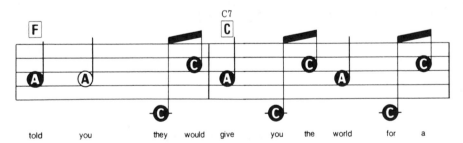

told   you   they   would   give   you   the   world   for   a

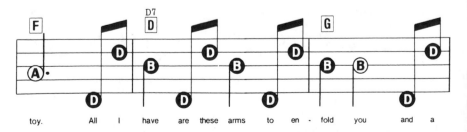

toy.   All   I   have   are   these   arms   to   en - fold   you   and   a

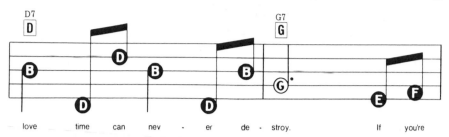

love time can nev - er de - stroy.   If you're

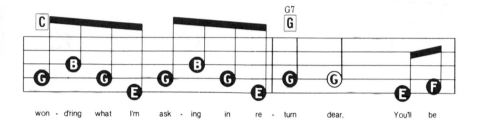

won - d'ring what I'm ask - ing in re - turn dear,   You'll be

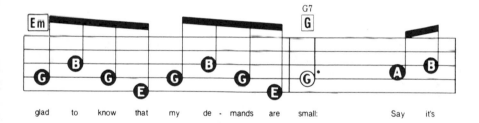

glad to know that my de - mands are small: Say it's

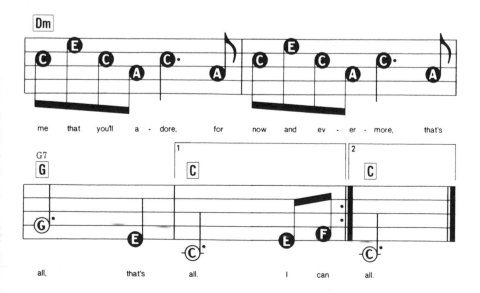

me that you'll a - dore,   for now and ev - er - more,   that's

all,   that's all.   I can all.

The River Seine
(La Seine)

Registration 2
Rhythm: Waltz

Words and Music by Allan Roberts and Alan Holt
Original French Text by Flavien Monod and Guy LaFarge

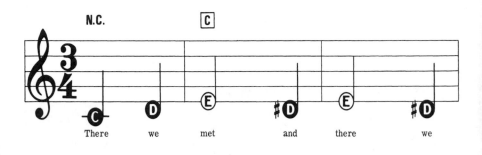

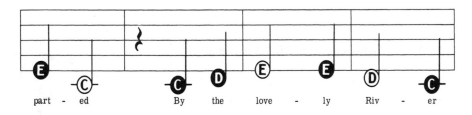

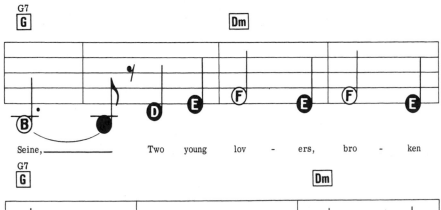

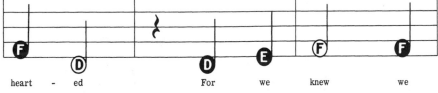

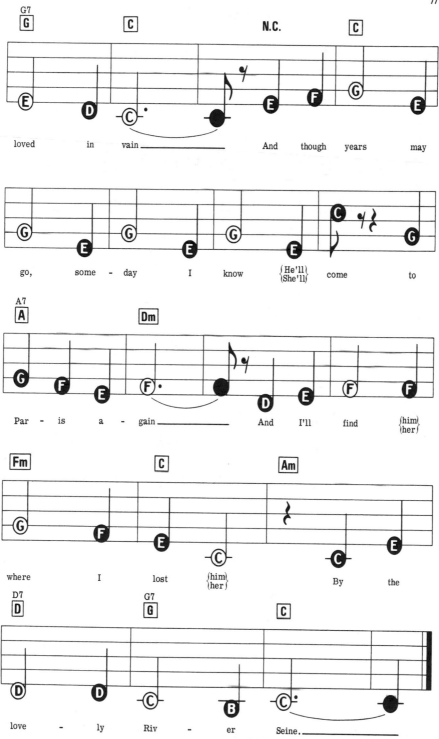

loved   in   vain _____   And   though   years   may

go,   some - day   I   know   {He'll}{She'll}   come   to

Par - is   a - gain _____   And   I'll   find   {him}{her}

where   I   lost   {him}{her}   By   the

love - ly   Riv - er   Seine. _____

Ruby

Registration 2
Rhythm: Swing

Music by Heinz Roemheld
Words by Mitchell Parish

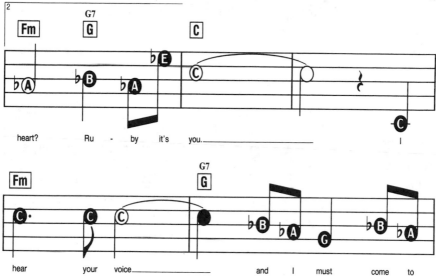

heart? Ru - by it's you._____ I

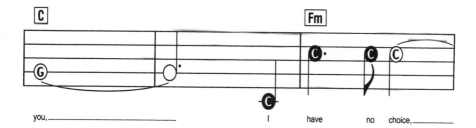

hear your voice_____ and I must come to

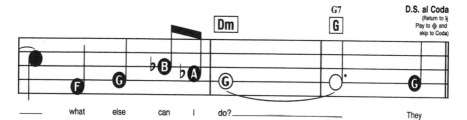

you,_____ I have no choice,_____

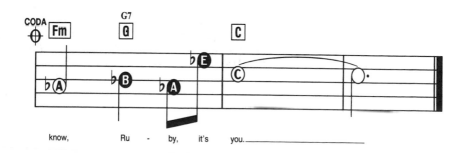

what else can I do?_____ They

know, Ru - by, it's you._____

Singin' in the Rain

Registration 4
Rhythm: Swing

Lyric by Arthur Freed
Music by Nacio Herb Brown

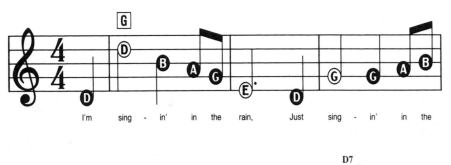

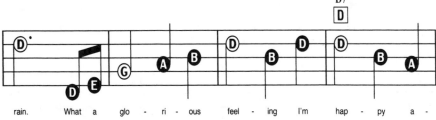

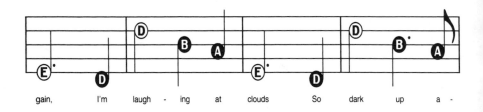

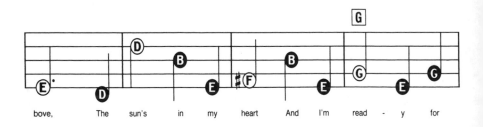

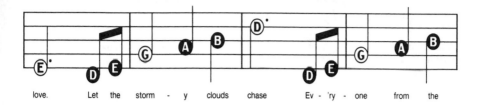

love. Let the storm - y clouds chase Ev - 'ry - one from the

D7
D

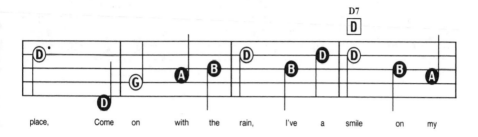

place, Come on with the rain, I've a smile on my

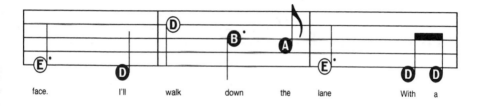

face. I'll walk down the lane With a

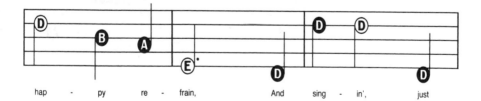

hap - py re - frain, And sing - in', just

G

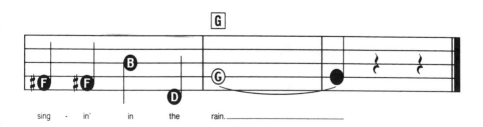

sing - in' in the rain.

Street of Dreams

Registration 1
Rhythm: Ballad or Fox Trot

Words and Music by Sam M. Lewis
and Victor Young

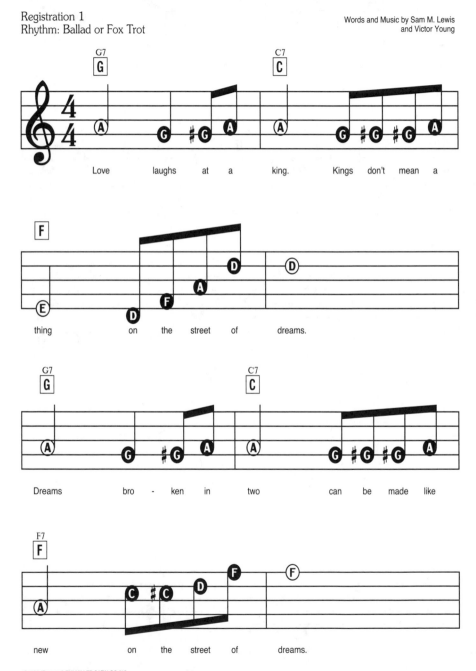

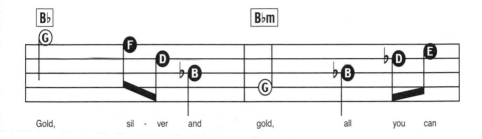

Gold, sil - ver and gold, all you can

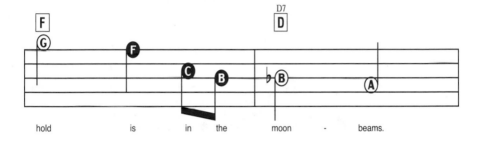

hold is in the moon - beams.

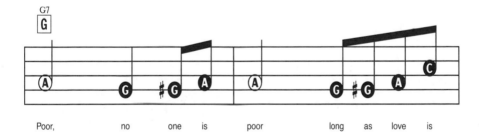

Poor, no one is poor long as love is

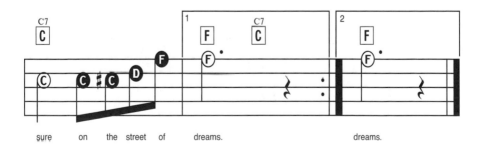

sure on the street of dreams. dreams.

Sunny

Registration: 3
Rhythm: Fox Trot or Ballad

Words and Music by
Bobby Hebb

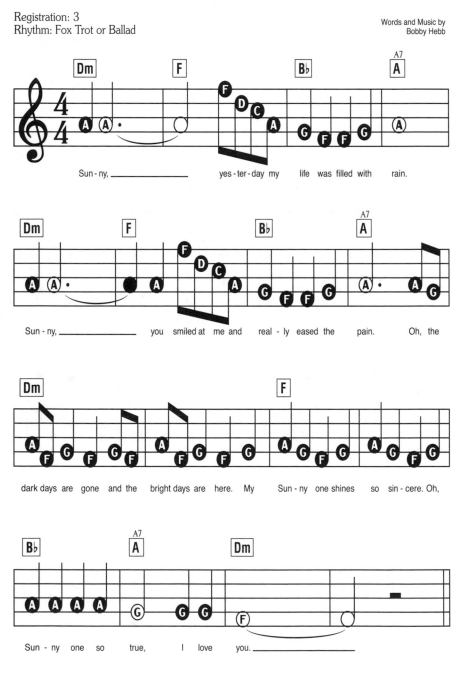

85

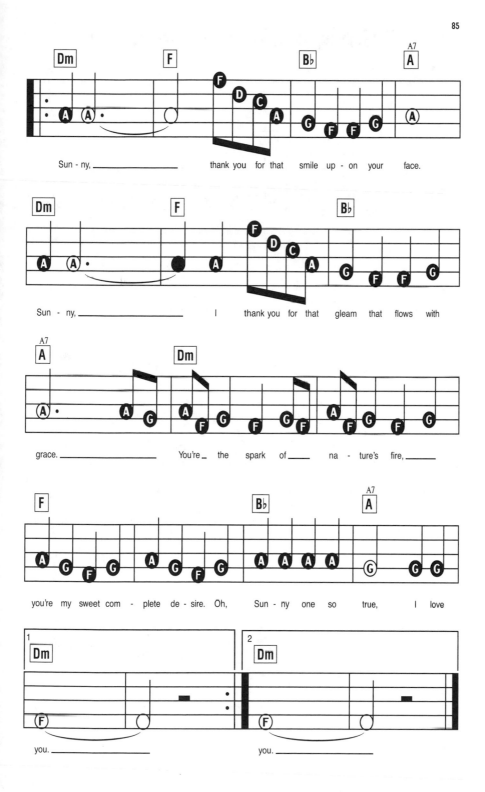

Taking a Chance on Love

Registration 7
Rhythm: Fox Trot or Swing

Words by John La Touche and Ted Fetter
Music by Vernon Duke

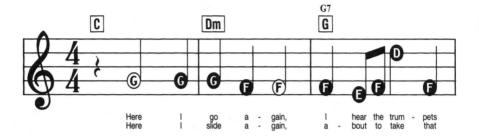

Here I go a - gain, I hear the trum - pets
Here I slide a - gain, a - bout to take that

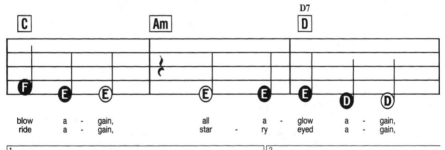

blow a - gain, all a - glow a - gain,
ride a - gain, star - ry eyed a - gain,

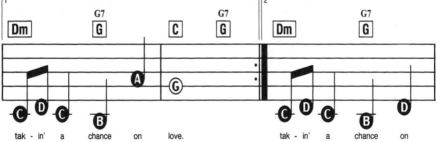

tak - in' a chance on love.
tak - in' a chance on

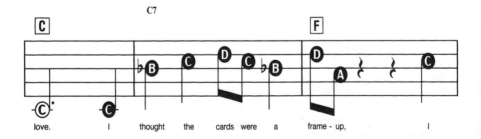

love. I thought the cards were a frame - up, I

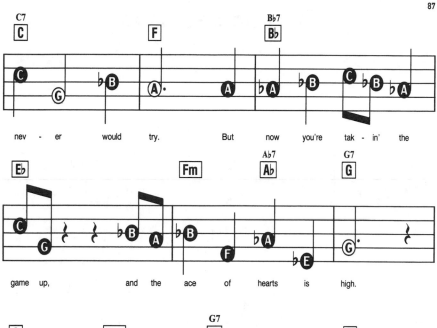

nev - er would try. But now you're tak - in' the

game up, and the ace of hearts is high.

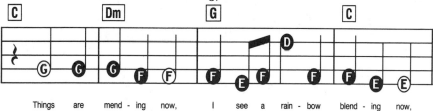

Things are mend - ing now, I see a rain - bow blend - ing now,

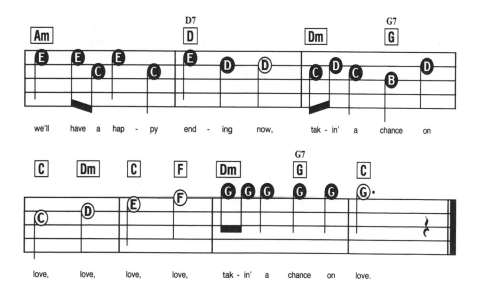

we'll have a hap - py end - ing now, tak - in' a chance on

love, love, love, love, tak - in' a chance on love.

A Time for Love

Registration 7
Rhythm: Swing or Jazz

Music by Johnny Mandel
Words by Paul Francis Webster

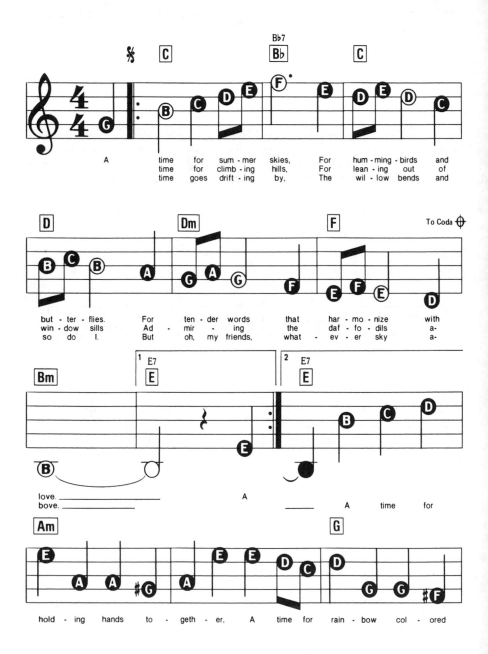

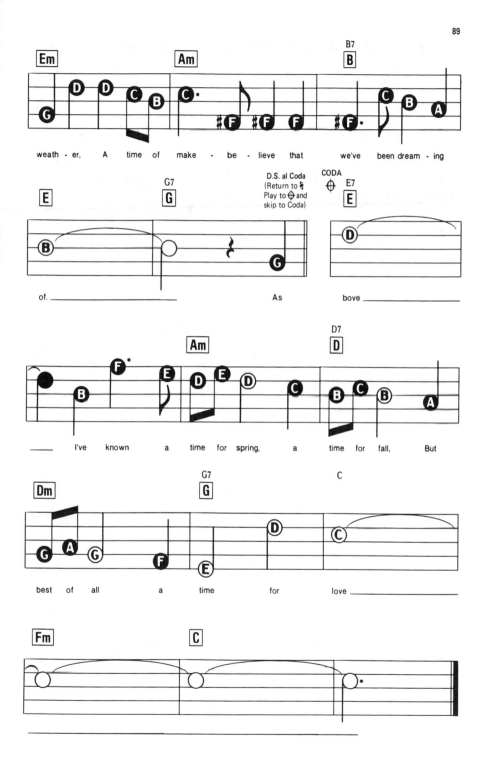

Tip-Toe Thru' the Tulips with Me

Registration 2
Rhythm: Swing or Jazz

Words by Al Dubin
Music by Joe Burke

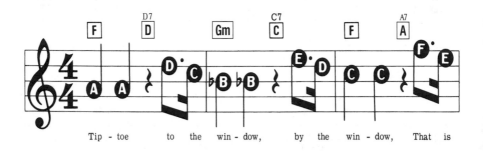

Tip - toe   to the win - dow,   by the   win - dow,   That is

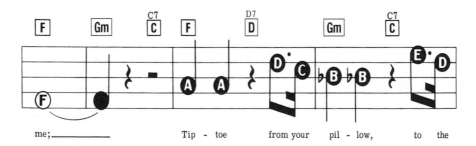

where   I'll   be,   Come   tip - toe   thru   the   tu - lips   with

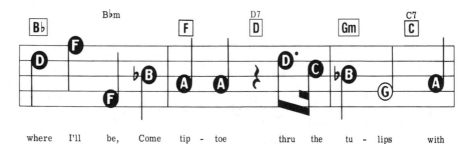

me;_____   Tip - toe   from your   pil - low,   to   the

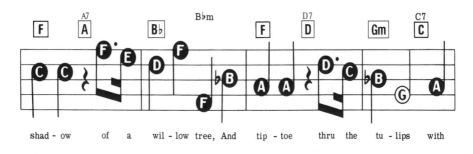

shad - ow   of   a   wil - low tree,   And   tip - toe   thru the   tu - lips   with

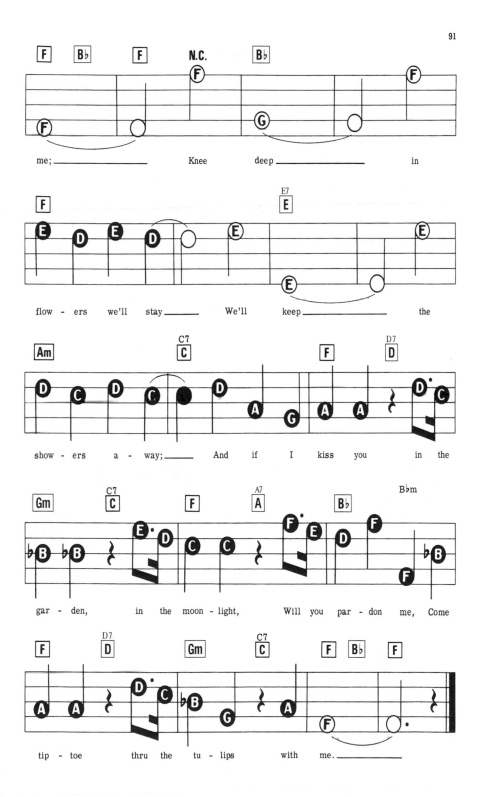

Walk On By

Registration 4
Rhythm: Rock, Pops, or Bossa Nova

Lyric by Hal David
Music by Burt Bacharach

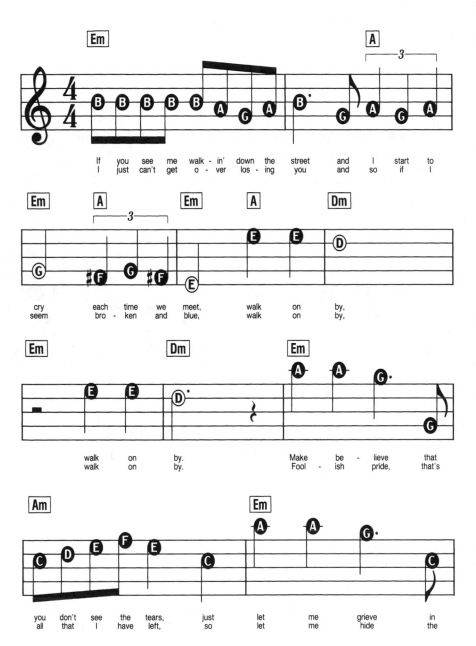

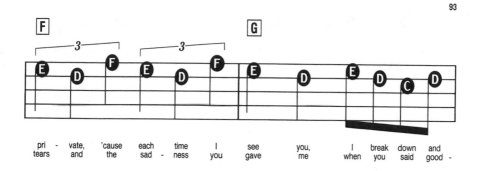

pri - vate, 'cause each time I see you, I break down and
tears and the sad - ness you gave me when you said good -

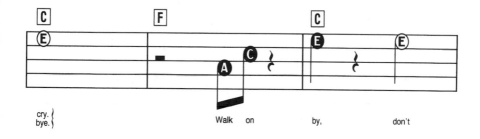

cry.
bye.　Walk on by, don't

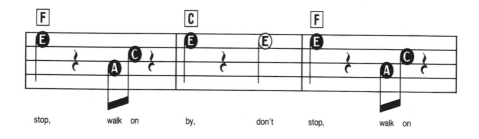

stop, walk on by, don't stop, walk on

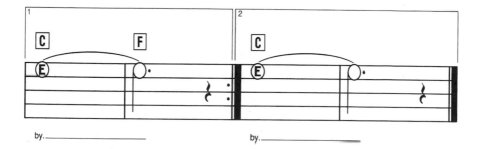

by.＿＿＿＿＿＿ by.＿＿＿＿＿＿

We're in This Love Together

Registration 4
Rhythm: Swing or Shuffle

Words and Music by Keith Stegall
and Roger Murrah

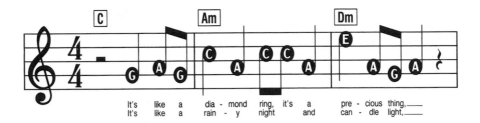

It's like a dia - mond ring, it's a pre - cious thing, ___
It's like a rain - y night and can - dle light, ___

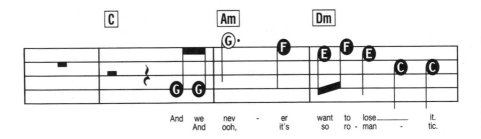

And we nev - er want to lose___ it.
And ooh, it's so ro - man - tic.

We got the whole___ thing work - ing___

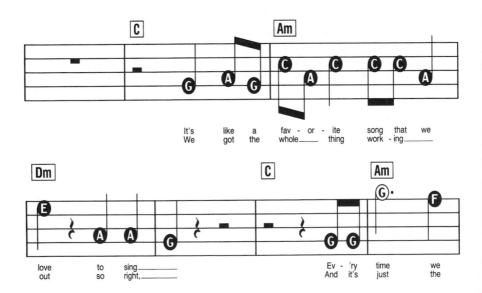

It's like a fav - or - ite song that we
We got the whole___ thing work - ing___

love to sing___ Ev - 'ry time we
out so right,___ And it's just the

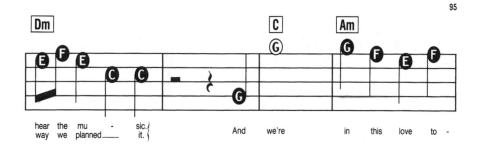

hear the mu - sic.
way we planned____ it.
And we're in this love to -

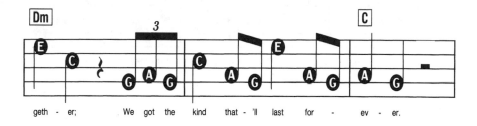

geth - er; We got the kind that - 'll last for - ev - er.

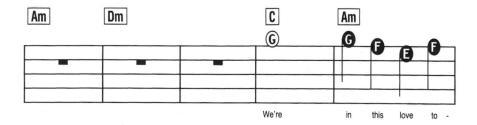

We're in this love to -

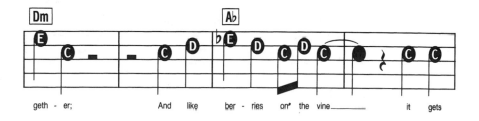

geth - er; And like ber - ries on* the vine____ it gets

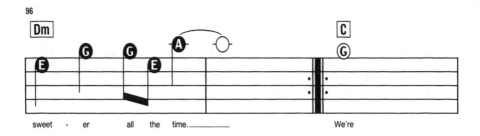

sweet - er   all   the   time._____   We're

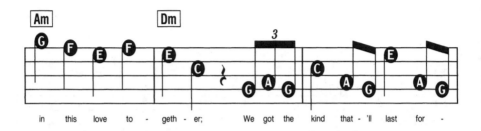

in   this   love   to - geth - er;   We got the   kind   that - 'll   last   for -

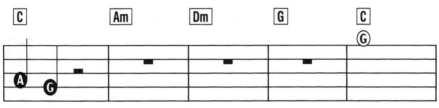

ev - er.   We're

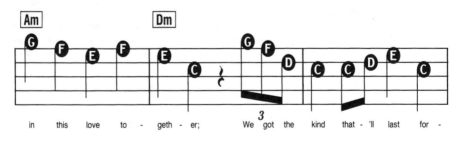

in   this   love   to - geth - er;   We got   the   kind   that - 'll   last   for -

Repeat and Fade

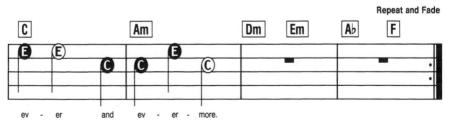

ev - er   and   ev - er - more.

When a Man Loves a Woman

Registration 4
Rhythm: Waltz or Slow Rock

Words and Music by Calvin Lewis
and Andrew Wright

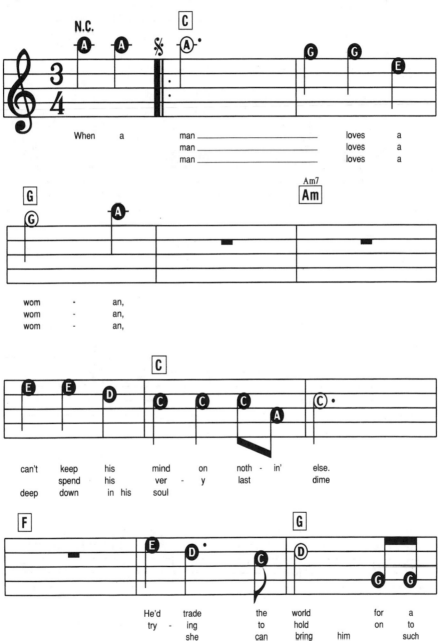

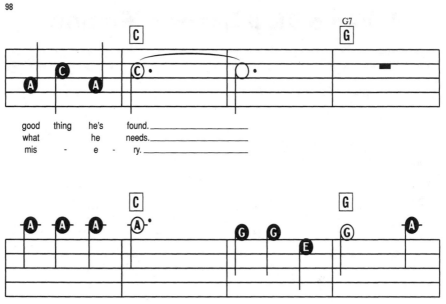

good thing   he's   found. _____
what   he   needs. _____
mis - e - ry. _____

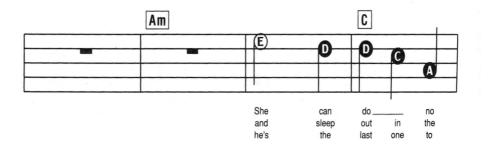

If   she   is   bad _____   he   can't   see   it.
He'd give   up   all _____   his   com -   forts
If   she   is   play - ing   him   for   a   fool, _____

She   can   do _____   no
and   sleep   out   in   the
he's   the   last   one   to

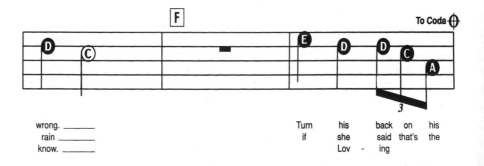

wrong. _____
rain _____
know. _____

Turn   his   back   on   his
        if   she   said   that's the
        Lov - ing

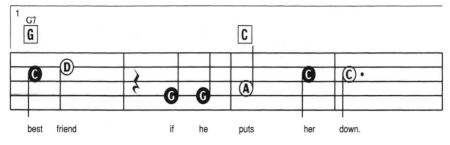

best friend   if   he   puts   her   down.

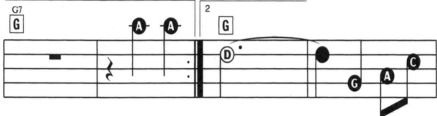

When a   way _____ it ought to

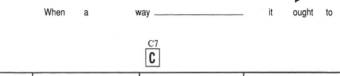

be.

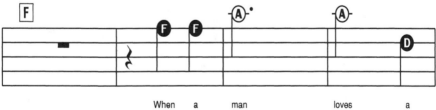

When a   man   loves   a

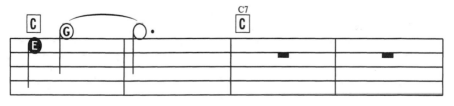

wom - an, _____

100

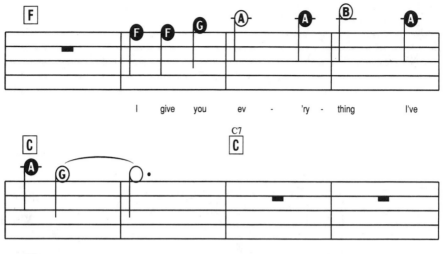

I give you ev - 'ry - thing I've

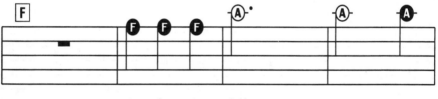
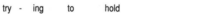

got, _____

try - ing to hold on to

your pre - cious love. _____

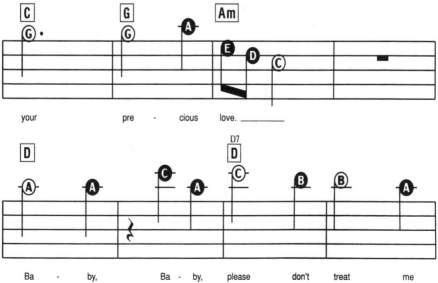

Ba - by, Ba - by, please don't treat me

101

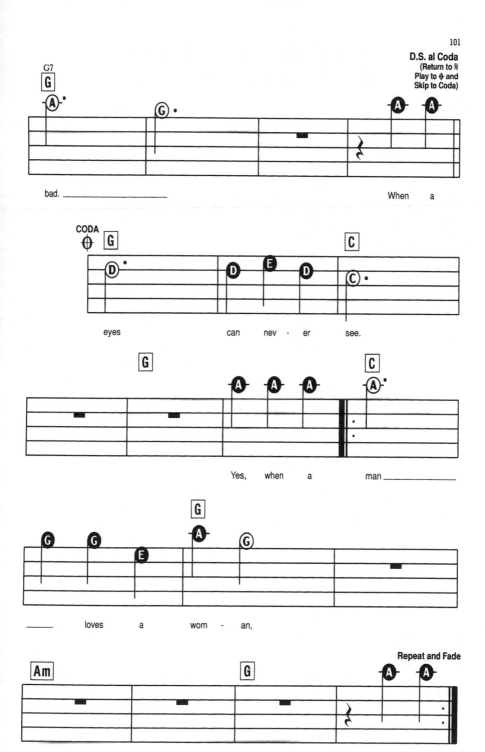

What Are You Doing the Rest of Your Life?

Registration 2
Rhythm: Bossa or Rock

Lyrics by Alan and Marilyn Bergman
Music by Michel Legrand

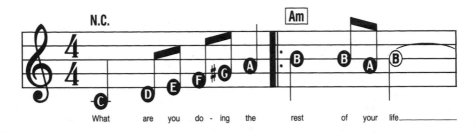

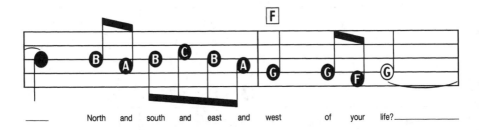

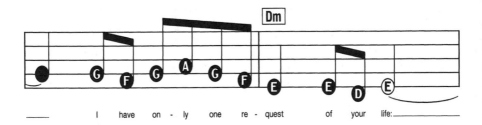

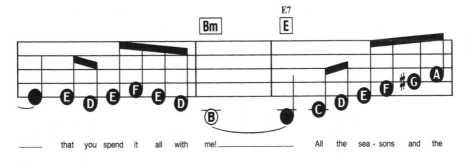

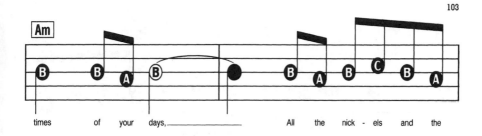

times   of   your   days,_____   All   the   nick - els   and   the

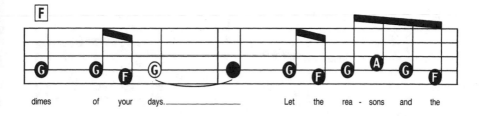

dimes   of   your   days._____   Let   the   rea - sons   and   the

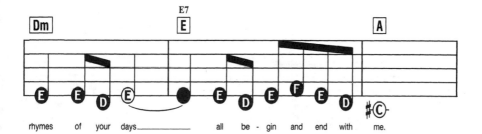

rhymes   of   your   days_____   all   be - gin   and   end   with   me.

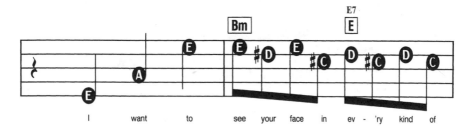

I   want   to   see   your   face   in   ev - 'ry   kind   of

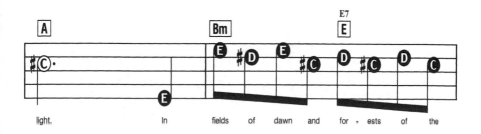

light,   In   fields   of   dawn   and   for - ests   of   the

104

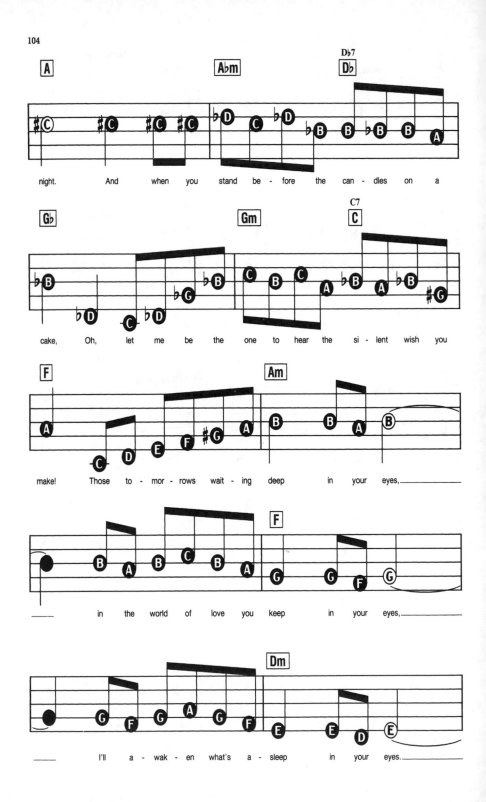

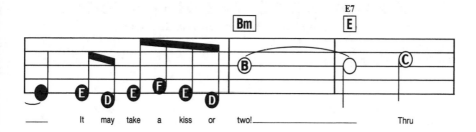

It may take a kiss or two! _____ Thru

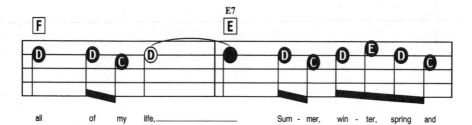

all of my life, _____ Sum - mer, win - ter, spring and

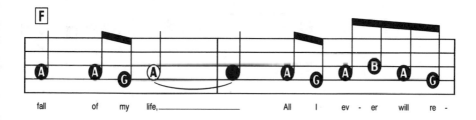

fall of my life, _____ All I ev - er will re -

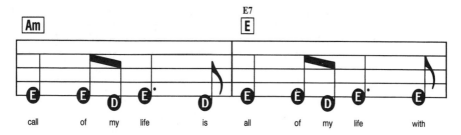

call of my life is all of my life with

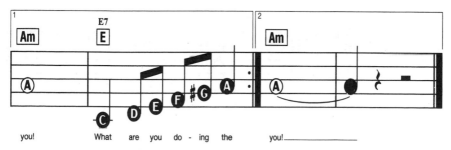

you! What are you do - ing the you! _____

You Stepped Out of a Dream

from the M-G-M Picture ZIEGFELD GIRL

Registration 7
Rhythm: Bossa Nova or Pops

Words by Gus Kahn
Music by Nacio Herb Brown

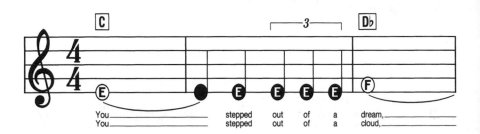

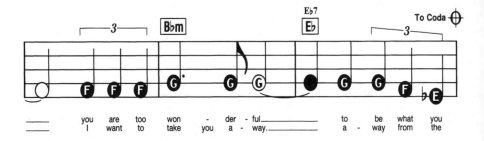

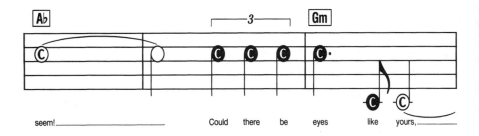

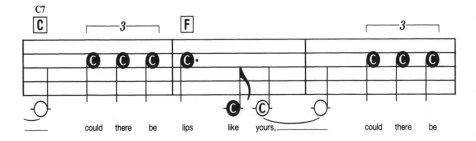

D.C. al Coda
(Return to beginning
Play to ⊕ and
skip to Coda)

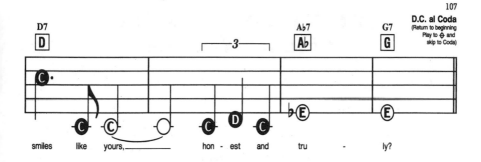

smiles like yours,_____ hon - est and tru - ly?

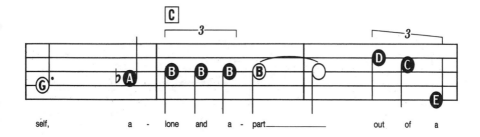

crowd,_____ and have you all to my -

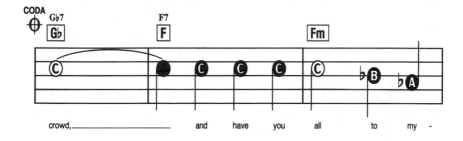

self, a - lone and a - part_____ out of a

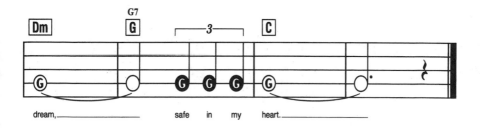

dream,_____ safe in my heart._____

You're Getting to Be a Habit With Me

Registration 8
Rhythm: Jazz or Swing

Lyrics by Al Dubin
Music by Harry Warren

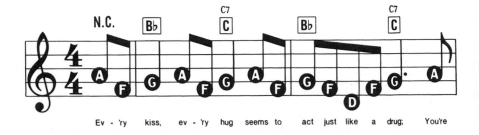

Ev - 'ry kiss, ev - 'ry hug seems to act just like a drug; You're

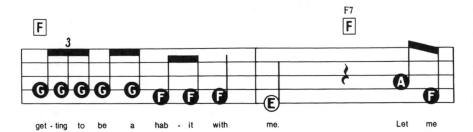

get - ting to be a hab - it with me. Let me

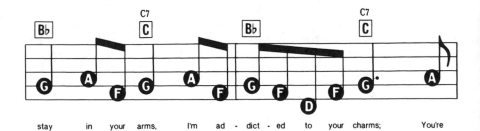

stay in your arms, I'm ad - dict - ed to your charms; You're

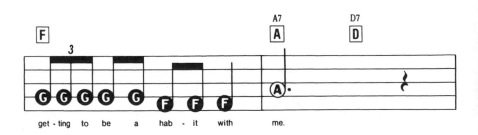

get - ting to be a hab - it with me.

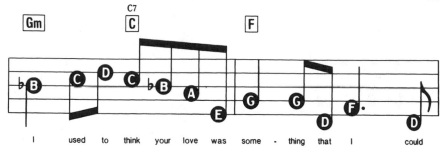

I used to think your love was some-thing that I could

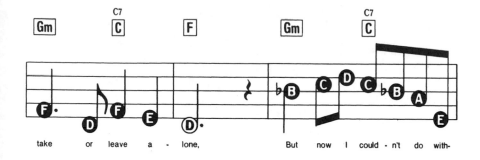

take or leave a-lone, But now I could-n't do with-

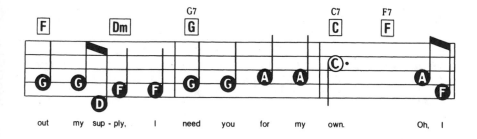

out my sup-ply, I need you for my own. Oh, I

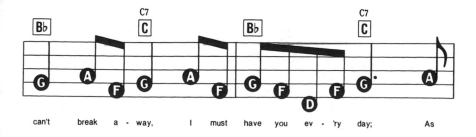

can't break a-way, I must have you ev-'ry day; As

110

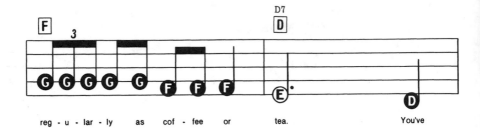

reg - u - lar - ly   as   cof - fee   or   tea.   You've

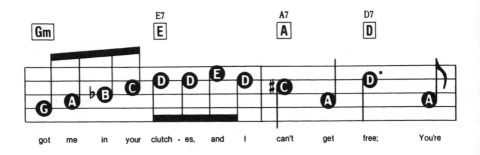

got   me   in   your   clutch - es,   and   I   can't   get   free;   You're

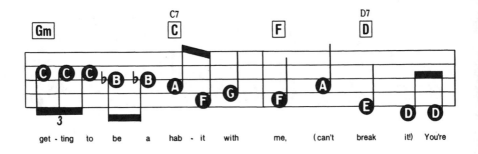

get - ting   to   be   a   hab - it   with   me,   (can't   break   it!)   You're

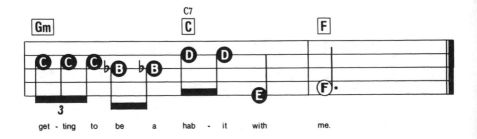

get - ting   to   be   a   hab - it   with   me.

Registration Guide

- Match the Registration number on the song to the corresponding numbered category below. Select and activate an instrumental sound available on your instrument.

- Choose an automatic rhythm appropriate to the mood and style of the song. (Consult your Owner's Guide for proper operation of automatic rhythm features.)

- Adjust the tempo and volume controls to comfortable settings.

Registration

1	Mellow	Flutes, Clarinet, Oboe, Flugel Horn, Trombone, French Horn, Organ Flutes
2	Ensemble	Brass Section, Sax Section, Wind Ensemble, Full Organ, Theater Organ
3	Strings	Violin, Viola, Cello, Fiddle, String Ensemble, Pizzicato, Organ Strings
4	Guitars	Acoustic/Electric Guitars, Banjo, Mandolin, Dulcimer, Ukulele, Hawaiian Guitar
5	Mallets	Vibraphone, Marimba, Xylophone, Steel Drums, Bells, Celesta, Chimes
6	Liturgical	Pipe Organ, Hand Bells, Vocal Ensemble, Choir, Organ Flutes
7	Bright	Saxophones, Trumpet, Mute Trumpet, Synth Leads, Jazz/Gospel Organs
8	Piano	Piano, Electric Piano, Honky Tonk Piano, Harpsichord, Clavi
9	Novelty	Melodic Percussion, Wah Trumpet, Synth, Whistle, Kazoo, Perc. Organ
10	Bellows	Accordion, French Accordion, Mussette, Harmonica, Pump Organ, Bagpipes